JEF

I'M READY

7 SIGNS

THAT SHOW YOU'RE RIGHT FOR THE JOB

I'm Ready: Seven signs that show you're right for the job
First published 2016 by Tangent Books

Tangent Books
Unit 5.16 Paintworks
Bristol BS4 3EH
0117 972 0645
www.tangentbooks.co.uk
Email: richard@tangentbooks.co.uk

ISBN 978-1-910089-48-4

By Jeff Mitchell

Edited by J M Lawrence (www.jmlawrence.co.uk)

Design: Joe Burt (joe@wildsparkdesign.com)

A CIP record of this book is available at the British Library.

DEDICATIONS

This book was brought into being through a crowdfunding campaign and made possible by the generous support of 77 backers. On their behalf, the book is dedicated to the following people:

Jim Divver
Karl Tucker
Jane de Vekey
Elizabeth Marshall
Ronald James Reed

The author dedicates *I'm Ready* to:

Jock, Steve, Barry, Simon and Simon

and all our kickstarters.

ACKNOWLEDGEMENTS

It has been a privilege to work with jobseekers like those in this book for the past ten years and all the people before who showed me what resilience is, slogging away day in, day out, despite being homeless, addicted, mentally ill or whatever.

Through this I've become a keen advocate of social enterprise, which is the business end of the spirit of enterprise found among people who'd otherwise be in line for handouts. On this note, my thanks go to John Bird, founder of The Big Issue, who reviewed this book but also taught me some key lessons about what it takes to make a success of the big challenges.

The crew at my social enterprise, Clean Slate, deserve total credit for delivering all that's described in this book and making my crazy ideas work when the whole world says it can't be done. All of you, from Work Champions to Directors, have my thanks, but especially Carole, Karina, Dan and Heloise.

This book wouldn't have been possible without the faith of Steve Faragher at the Social Publishing Project. Thanks to Joe on design, Richard at Tangent Books and Jamie the editor, whose patience, support and positive attitude helped smooth the horribly rough edges of the first drafts of this book.

Finally, thanks to the crowdfunding backers (and Dave Harvey for spreading the word), and of course family and friends who know when to get behind me and when to laugh in my face.

Jeff Mitchell, 2016

CONTENTS

SIGN 6: PRESENTATION

SIGN 7: MOTIVATION

20 NEXT STEPS FOR JOBSEEKERS

MOVING ON

WELCOME TO SEVEN SIGNS TRAINING

Meet Jock, Naz, Ali, Ying and Antonio. They've been out of work for a while and each one is trying to throw off their own demons.

They've had it tough and don't think they have much in common until they start to look at themselves through employers' eyes. With a little direction and the chance to prove how much they have to offer, things start to change.

How many will make it to the point of saying "I'm ready?"

This is a book designed to help jobseekers but it's not a 'how to' guide or some kind of 'jobseeking for dummies' manual.

It's the story of a few people I've met over the past ten years at my social enterprise, Clean Slate Training & Employment. It follows their progress through highs and lows, triumph and tragedy. We watch them work towards their ultimate goal – taking back control of their lives and proudly standing on their own two feet.

The characters are a mash up of real people who have joined us along the way but Jock was my starting point in this story. In many ways, he was the starting point for Clean Slate because if anyone needed a 'clean slate' it was him.

He was one of the first people that taught me you can't tell how much someone has to offer by where they sleep at night, what medication they're on, or what they've done in the past. Watching him grow from beggar to one of the hardest working people I've ever known changed my outlook forever.

At Clean Slate we've met over 5,000 jobless people. About 2,000 have followed the Seven Signs training that you'll go through by reading this book. I've watched their eyes light up as they realise how a new approach might just lead to success.

We know one in five find work directly after taking our Seven Signs training and receiving the support that comes with it. We reckon at least the same number again are inspired to find help with the things outside jobseeking that are holding them back in life.

Many don't succeed first time but they'll come round again when they're ready. Others go on, at their own pace, to discover that what they needed to get ahead was within them the whole time.

So come and meet the crew as we follow their stories. Look on as Jock overcomes homelessness, Naz puts his troubled past to use and Ali discovers her life as a young parent might actually be the source of new job options.

Join our group and see how the Seven Signs, when switched on, tell employers you're not only ready for the job but could be the new star of their organisation.

Near the end of the book, we've included our 20 Next Steps for Jobseekers. Our jobseekers in the story receive a copy and you can work through it if you want in the real world. If you're online, you can also find more ideas and hidden extras on our website, at www.7signs.org.uk.

Nothing would be a more fitting tribute to the people that inspired *I'm Ready* than for you, or someone you share these ideas with, to stand up and say to an employer those two words: "I'm ready!"

Jeff Mitchell, 2016

A CLEAN SLATE

The favour

Jock was begging on the street when Rich approached him about a new employment project. Jock looked at him through dewy eyes caused by that morning's bellyful of cheap cider.

The sun was bright and he held his hand to his forehead for shade. Rich was about the last person he expected to see. He stared toothlessly back at him.

"You got a screw loose or something? You do remember who I am?"

"Take it or leave it," Rich replied. "There's work there if you want it."

"Aye. Whatever."

"Seriously. Are you free tomorrow at all?'

Jock looked around sarcastically. "What do you think?" He felt he should stand up. Rich was over six feet tall and leaning over him, but Jock was worried his legs wouldn't hold him up.

"I didn't mean to be funny," Rich said matter-offactly. "It's just I've got 10,000 condoms on my desk… no, seriously…"

He explained the local council had asked him to put a team together to pack sexual health kits for every clinic in the city.

"I have five people lined up already but I could do with a couple more."

"Nah, I don't think so."

"Why not?"

"I cannae work. Look at the state of me."

"Do you think there's a dress code?"

"No, but…" Jock swallowed, looking up and down the street. He was trying to find something, some escape, someone who could interrupt the conversation. This was all too familiar.

He looked back to Rich. "We've been here before."

Rich held his eyes. "So? There's a lot of water under the bridge. If I'm honest, I want to wipe the slate clean on that. Come on, let's help each other out."

"You don't need drinkers like me. I can't work."

"All I care about is getting those 10,000 condoms into little paper bags. I can't have you drinking on the job but as far as I'm concerned there are plenty of people in full-time work in posh offices around the city that can't go the day without a drink. So why can't I have you putting those kits together?"

Rich paused. Jock was looking down at the pavement now. He'd given up on finding an escape. Rich could tell he was thinking about it.

"I'll need you working to speed as we're not getting paid a lot to do it and I need you to be safe but you'll really be helping me out."

"Well," Jock said slowly, "if it would help you out…"

"It would. And you'll get paid by the hour."

"I might not be able to do the whole day."

"You'll get paid for whatever you work."

"I'm not worried about the money."

"But it's important to me. The customer's paying us so you have to get paid. Actually, do you know anyone else who might want some work?"

"Really?"

"Sure. They just need to be able to work hard and be safe. That's all I care about. No monkeying about."

Rich explained that if anyone was on welfare, they'd need to declare their earnings to the Job Centre. Jock, though, had stopped signing on a few weeks after being released from jail, when they had threatened to suspend his claim. Taking handouts on the streets just seemed easier.

"The point is, it's work. It's better than sitting around in the cold, and it'll be helping me out."

Jock rubbed his hands together, blew on them and nodded.

"See you tomorrow, Jock. A clean slate. Remember that."

The next day Jock arrived fifteen minutes early. Rich had also just arrived and asked Jock to unpack the stock and set up small stations around a large room.

Three others arrived by 9am, a deadline Rich had deliberately set to test the workers' motivation. He made it clear he noticed when they arrived.

One looked like he was about to fall asleep any moment and another looked like his hair hadn't seen a brush in 20 years. But it didn't matter – they were here and they'd get the job done.

"Okay, guys, for those of you who haven't worked for us before, I just want to spell out how this works. Today, we're your employer but there's more to us than that. Yes, we want to give you a break and help you make money… legally. Work hard and we'll put as much work your way as we can."

Rich paused to check everyone was tuned into what he was saying, then continued.

"But we're not-for-profit and whatever we make is ploughed into a training course called Seven Signs, so you can progress from this work today to wherever it is you really should be working. When you realise you can do much more than the work you're doing today, we want you on our training course. It's just two hours a week and will change the way you look at yourself and your prospects."

This was news to Jock. The course sounded like something for other people but it felt good to know. He smiled to himself. He should have guessed there was more to this than met the eye. He knew Rich better. He hadn't changed.

"Jock, can I have a quick word?" Rich said.

The pair of them stepped outside briefly and when they returned, Rich announced that Jock would oversee the job.

Jock checked everyone had the stock they needed and made a round of hot drinks. Rich returned at 11am with a late arrival.

Jock agreed it was okay for Naz to join the team, but he added: "I'm not sure how much there is left to do, mind. We're all steaming through, aren't we guys?"

Naz noticed the team wasn't very welcoming but figured this was their problem. Rich also noticed the frosty reception. *Here's your first lesson straight from the team,* he thought. *Arrive at the start time and people will make you feel welcome.*

At the end of the day, Rich collected the time sheets from Jock. A couple of boxes of stock still remained and Jock had already lined up the reliable workers for the following day. Rich was made up.

"Jock, that's great. On your timesheet, I want you to change the hourly rate you're claiming to the supervisor rate."

"Eh? What for?"

"That's the job you were doing. You should be paid for it. Without you, I'd have had to sit there all day instead of making these calls and sending off emails. This was a much better use of my time, in all honesty."

He was surprised that Jock was reluctant to be paid more than the rest of the team but Rich just reminded Jock this was how businesses work.

As Jock opened the door to leave, he stopped, looking sheepish.

"Erm, thanks for today."

"No, I want to thank you."

"You know what I mean."

"And you know what I mean. Clean slate, remember? See you tomorrow."

As the door closed, Rich wondered how Jock had coped without drink. He was still coherent, even at 5.30, and didn't seem to have had a drop. He'd got the job done. That was all that mattered. Hopefully he'd do the same tomorrow.

Ready for the next step?

Two months later, Jock was having coffee with Rich. They'd started meeting regularly after the first packing job.

There was just a skylight window in Rich's office and the walls were hidden behind racking stuffed with archive crates, boxes full of leaflets and old computer equipment.

"Sorry there hasn't been more work, mate."

"Ah, it's been fine. I know you're just getting going. I've earnt almost as much as I wouldda on benefits. Three weeks out of four."

"It's almost two months now, isn't it?"

"Never. I take no notice." Jock was properly shocked. He thought about it. "Aye, I think you're right."

"I wanted to ask if you'd thought any more about finding more regular work. If you're ready." Rich held Jock's eyes. "Are you ready?"

"Who's gonna employ me?"

Rich continued to look into Jock's eyes but didn't speak, slowly sipping his coffee. Jock thought Rich was composing his answer. Perhaps he agreed that no-one would take him on. Then he noticed Rich tilt his head with the tiniest of movements, suddenly smiling.

"Oh, aye, okay. Well, apart from you. That's different."

"Why's it different?"

Jock paused. He realised he didn't really have an answer. "Because, erm, this is what you do?"

"What do I do?"

"Help people like me. With work opportunities and training."

"Really? You do a job and we pay you." Rich was no longer smiling.

"Yeah, but for people like me."

"Don't you do a good job? Don't you earn your money? Or do you still think you're doing me a favour?"

"Ha." Jock thought back to the day on the street when Rich asked him if he wanted work. "I did honestly think I was helping you out but I forgot that the minute I picked up my wages."

"I had to do something to get you in through the door. You didn't believe in yourself but I did. It's interesting. Why do I have faith in you and not the guys you hang around with in the park? You'd think that if I can find work for *some* rough sleepers, I could employ anyone. Why do so few let me down?

"People don't let me down *because* they're homeless. They only let me down when they're not the right person for that job, at that time. Once I got that straight, the doors opened to everyone from every group that recruiters put on the reject pile without thinking.

"It's helped me understand the processes all employers use. Not the ones they are conscious of. There's a whole load of stuff they look at that isn't relevant…"

"Like where you sleep," Jock said.

"Yeah, exactly," said Rich. "We have to guide people along because what really messes me about is when people aren't clear what they want to do.

"What do I care if someone says 'no' to cleaning a customer's windows because they don't want to work out in the cold? I'll find someone who will. But if someone says they will and then they let me down, then I care. And I will probably feel less inclined to help them find the work they do want.

"What I think we do here, at this company, is boil things down to just what matters. There are signs we look for in people like you. Seven of them, in fact. The things you'd never say, Jock, but that shout out to me 'I'm ready!'"

"What, even when I was begging?" asked Jock.

"Well, that was a hunch but when you turned up the

next day, I knew. It's those Seven Signs that will allow you to move on from here. Get another job. Do what you really want to do."

Jock looked at the floor. "So what are the signs?"

Rich smiled. "You need to meet Cheryl. She runs our Seven Signs training."

Tame your snakes and build your ladders

Cheryl was shorter than everyone else in the room and spoke with a strong Bristolian accent. Jock tried not to laugh but she sounded like a pirate. She handed out black stickers and marker pens and asked everyone to write a name badge and stick it on their t-shirt.

She explained how the programme ran over four sessions, once a fortnight. The idea was to work together to see what everyone had to offer. They'd learn to display the Seven Signs that show employers they're ready, and right, for the job.

She took her place next to a flipchart stand that was taller than she was. Everyone sat down in chairs facing her. Some were younger and Jock thought they looked defensive and awkward. Some were older, waiting to be impressed but without much hope they would be.

Tough crowd, Jock thought to himself. One guy had a scraggy beard and jeans he held up with his hands. The homeless stereotype. *Just like me a few months ago.*

Cheryl eyed everyone from the front of the room. "Let's play a game."

Naz looked down at the floor. "No. Let's not."

"Thank you, Naz," said Cheryl, looking at him. "I should warn you I have bat-like hearing."

She drew a big, square grid on the flipchart. It was ten squares wide and ten squares high and each square was numbered one to 100. She reached into her work bag and groped about for a moment.

"Okay, so here we have some snakes," she said, holding up two fluffy snakes in her right hand. In her left hand were a couple of plastic ladders. "And here are the ladders. Who hasn't played Snakes and Ladders?"

A few people looked unsure. Cheryl always made a point never to assume everyone had the same knowledge. It was a mixed group that could include people from other countries, those with learning disabilities, those with mental health problems or people on drugs and alcohol programmes.

Everyone would be at different stages on their journey back to work. The snakes and ladders looked weird to some people. But she hoped they would be patient and open-minded. The ones who were ready to work always were.

Cheryl asked those who knew Snakes and Ladders to explain the rules. A young woman called Ying started talking, trying to make a good first impression.

"Players take turns to roll the dice and move along the board starting at square one and working towards 100. The first one to get to square 100 is the winner. Along the way, there are a couple of ladders."

She smiled at Cheryl, who stuck a few ladders onto the grid.

"Some ladders are long," said Ying, "so if you roll a five and land on square five, you go up the ladder to square 65. Other ladders are shorter. If you land on square 10 you'll only go up to square 21 on that ladder that Cheryl put on the flipchart."

She paused as Cheryl stuck two snakes on the flipchart, then continued. "Okay, so you also need to beware that if you land on a snake, they drag you back down the board… from, let's see, number 67 back to number four.'

"That's harsh," Naz joked. Cheryl looked up and he continued. "I'm just saying that you could strike lucky with that big old ladder, end up on square 65 and then roll a two, then you're further back than you were before."

"Aha," Cheryl said. "Life's a bitch, right? Has anyone here felt like they've stepped on a snake and gone backwards?" Every hand went up. "Yep, thought so, everyone."

"Sorta," Jock mumbled. "I brought it on myself, but yeah."

"Interesting point, Jock," Cheryl replied.

"Did you really, though?" said Naz. "Sometimes we blame ourselves for things we have no control over."

"And sometimes we blame others for things we could have done something about," Ying countered.

Cheryl stepped in. "Okay, okay. You're all stealing

my thunder here. I was just about to ask how the game is different from real life."

Naz drew breath to speak but Cheryl shot him a look with a smile and kept talking.

"Life is not like rolling a dice. It's not always a game of chance. Sometimes we're just plain unlucky but other times we could do more to make our own luck."

Cheryl paused and pointed to the flipchart, with the snakes and ladders still stuck to the paper. "I believe that in life we can do more to avoid the bad squares and work towards the good ones. Do you agree?"

"Like building our own ladders?" Ying asked.

"Exactly like that. And taming our snakes," Cheryl added. "That's what I'm going to show you. Well, that's what you're going to show each other. You already know this stuff, you just don't realise it."

"How can you know that? You don't know us," Naz challenged.

"Because we're here, ya muppet," Jock said impatiently. "They invited 25 people to Seven Signs training. We're the ones who stepped up. Even you."

As one of the few she'd met before, Cheryl asked if Jock would be prepared to share with the group what the big snakes in his life were. He named booze, his criminal record and sleeping rough, although he was currently staying on a friend's floor.

Ying was thinking about the snakes in her life. She had been referred to Seven Signs training by a mental health charity called Mindspace. They had helped her get back on top since losing her father 18 months earlier.

Having given up studies and work to care for him through his long illness, she'd felt lost and alone and unable to support her mother after he'd died. The days when she just didn't want to get out of bed were now rare but often, before going to sleep, she was terrified of how she'd feel the following morning.

She imagined the snakes with fangs, injecting venom that made her feel numb, lifeless and unable to face the day.

Cheryl was looking round the room. "Many courses you go on will talk about ways to overcome the things holding you back but we're not going to focus on those things here. I think if you dwell on the negative too much, you give it power. Instead, we're going to focus on the ladders we can build for ourselves and the luck we can make for ourselves. How does that sound?" The room was silent. "Ali?"

Alison had not spoken and had not even been noticed by most of the group. Her eyes were looking at the floor. She was not thinking about the course.

She was thinking about the meeting she was due to have later with her new landlord, about her rent arrears. She was wondering how her daughter was doing at the school she'd only started last week, and growing anxious that she wouldn't make it in time to pick her up after today's training.

She realised everyone was looking at her and

mumbled something.

"Sorry, Ali, my bat ears are failing me. You're going to have to help me out and speak up. Are you up for building some ladders to get you into a job?"

"I s'pose."

"Okay, it's hard to imagine, but I've done this training quite a few times now and if you see it through, we'll get you there. The first thing we'll want to do is work out where your ladders are supposed to be reaching towards. And we'll need to decide what's in your square 100. That's where the hedgehog lives." Her eyes twinkled. "Ah, yes, more on him later.

"But let's just capture where we are now. What's holding you all back? Jock's named his snakes. I want you all to do the same. Jot them down and think about all the things you can do to try to avoid them or minimise the harm they can do to you, if you step on them."

Jock had already named his snakes but it was harder to think about what he might do to keep them at bay. After ten minutes he'd come up with a few basic ideas:

- Keep busy
- Set times of the day to stay off the drink
- Hang out less with other drinkers
- Think twice before I act
- Take pride
- Apply for a hostel place
- Re-apply for benefits

- Make some money
- Keep money safe

Jock stared at the list and realised it was already a work in progress. *These are rungs on my ladder,* he thought. *I've already started doing some of these, so I'm already a couple of steps up.*

He smiled to himself and looked around to see how everyone else was getting on.

I'M READY

SIGN 1: WHAT EMPLOYERS WANT

Are all employers judgemental?

"Stand up," Cheryl said, grinning broadly. "No more games. Time to get some energy into the room."

She wrote the word 'AGREE' on a sheet of paper and stuck it to the wall on the right of the room. She wrote 'DISAGREE' on another piece of paper and stuck it to the left-hand wall.

"Stand on the right if you agree with the statement I'm about to say and on the left if you disagree. Ready? All employers are judgemental."

There was shuffling around. A few people looked surprised. They had expected the day to be spent listening to someone tell them what to do. And say. And think. Now they were being asked what they thought of employers. Weird. For Jock, there was only one thing to do – go along with it. He stood as close to the 'AGREE' sign as he could.

Cheryl asked him why he had chosen that side.

"Everyone's judgemental. When I was begging, everyone assumed I was good for nothing. Now I've done a bit of work for Rich, I'm still the same person. It's just how people are."

He continued. "That shouldnae mean I can't do a job but no-one was going to take me on looking like I did. If I started wearing smart clobber, a suit like, they'd be even more impressed but I'd *still* be the same person."

People nodded. There was a discussion about how fair, or not, that was. Some people saw it as prejudiced and others were pragmatic.

Jock sighed. "If it's human nature, we have to work around it."

Everyone was nodding. All except Antonio, who was still struggling to keep his trousers aloft. He started to speak in his broad French accent. "I'm sorry. What is 'clobber'?"

Jock burst out laughing and explained he meant his clothing. Cheryl went round the room, asking people their opinions and building a conversation, carefully pointing out that there was no right or wrong. All opinions were valid.

Soon everyone was seated again. Cheryl stood at the front.

"I'm not going to make you wear funny glasses but you're now going to look at yourselves through employers' eyes."

She divided the room into four teams of three and

introduced the session as a roleplay where each team would act as a recruitment panel. They were issued with a job description for a fictional post that needed filling, which was based on the helpdesk downstairs, where the bubbly receptionist called everyone 'my lurve.'

Then they were issued with a score sheet, listing six criteria the panel would be looking for. They would need to score three different jobseekers from 1-5 on each criteria. The six criteria were:

- This person is motivated
- This person wants the work we have on offer
- They are confident
- Communication skills
- Able to work in a team and under direction
- Organised

Finally, Cheryl circulated three short personal statements, one for each jobseeker.

Personal Statement 1: Steve

I am a likeable person looking for any kind of work and I don't care who I work for. I've been out of work for four years through no fault of my own and I don't want to be on the dole any more. I am looking for an employer to give me a chance.

Personal Statement 2: Maria
I am looking for office work where I can put my communication and people skills to use. Ideally I would like a customer service role, working towards a management position in a company committed to its service users and the wider community. Having overcome considerable life challenges, I am looking for the opportunity to grow in the world of work.

Personal Statement 3: Yusuf
As a keen gardener, I want to find outdoor work where I can use my organisational skills, patience and ability to work on my own. I am keen to work for an employer that would value my contribution and understands I've had a difficult past, which I've overcome through determination and hard work. I would work hard and be loyal.

The groups quickly set to work, talking and arguing about the merits of each candidate and what scores to put down against each of the criteria for all three candidates. Jock watched Cheryl wander around checking they had the right idea and listening in on the conversations.

When she came to Jock's team, they were in heated

debate about whether or not one candidate sounded like they had good interpersonal skills. Soon Cheryl brought everyone back together.

She drew a grid on a sheet of flipchart paper and filled in the different scores each team had given the three candidates.

Some teams had consistently lower scores for each one, while others were generous, but three of the four groups had agreed on who would be offered the job, who came second and who would perhaps be referred to Cheryl for some advice on how to impress employers better in future.

	Steve	Maria	Yusuf
Team 1	12	21	18
Team 2	20	23	22
Team 3	20	19	16
Team 4	11	15	14

"Some of you will make harsh bosses," she joked. "Boy, you have high standards. But what really matters here is that you agreed on who you'd take on.

"So Maria is most people's winner. Let's look at the other winner. Naz, why did your panel choose Steve?"

"Well, I have to be truthful, it was a split decision. I kind of put my foot down about this. I really thought Steve deserved a chance because he's been down on his luck through no fault of his own.

"Through no fault of his own," he re-emphasised. "He'd be so grateful, he'd repay you in loyalty even if he wasn't quite as good as Maria."

"No, no, no," Jock said forcefully. "You can't do that. It has to go to the best person for the job. And also, you have no way of knowing if it's not his fault he's unemployed. You can't take that into account."

Lots of people around the room were nodding their agreement as they had, after all, selected Maria.

"Is there anything wrong with taking on someone who would be grateful?" said Cheryl.

Ying put up her hand. "It's a bit patronising."

Cheryl asked Naz if he'd be happy being expected to feel grateful for a job offer.

"No way but *I* wouldn't be that desperate."

"By the end of this course, I hope you'll believe that no-one has any reason to feel grateful," said Cheryl.

"I want you to be able to tell an employer that you have what they want. An interview is not a trial or a tug of war. They're looking for someone with certain skills. You're offering certain skills. It would be a rubbish tug of war - they're pulling and you're pushing."

Cheryl saw a few people nodding in understanding.

"You'll be competing on a level playing field and no-one will owe anyone anything... except maybe some wages."

A few people laughed. At that moment the door opened and Rich came into the room. He perched on a table to the side of the flipchart stand and asked them all not to let him interrupt their discussion.

Cheryl asked the rest of the group why most of them had ranked Steve third.

Ying spoke up. "He didn't really say anything and actually sounded like he had a bit of a chip on his shoulder. He blamed everyone else for his situation. We thought that by saying he didn't mind anything, he could just as easily not want to do anything."

"That's what I thought," Cheryl said. She smiled at Rich. "I think this is where you come in."

Rich got up off the table and stood near Cheryl.

"Well," he said, "some of you have heard me say this before but for our organisation, there's no point taking on someone who says they'll do anything because I would put money on the fact that if I asked them to clean toilets, it'll turn out they would rather be working on computers. If I offered them office work, they'd want to work outdoors.

"Basically, we don't have time to put people into the wrong jobs or replace them when they get fed up and leave."

"That's why Yusuf didn't get our job," Jock offered, feeling confident with Rich there. "He sounded like a good employee. He seemed confident and knew what he wanted but he wouldnae be happy in an admin role. He wants to be doing what he enjoys, outside in the garden."

Cheryl asked if everyone could see how the process worked and if they'd noticed how it was human nature to read between the lines and form a picture, even when the information was incomplete.

"You've all gone quiet," she said. "Why so shy just because the boss is here? Guys, now is your time to pipe up, not down."

She thought it was interesting how the feel of the room had changed. Naz had folded his arms again. Alison stared at the floor and Ying was not so keen to offer anything.

Cheryl persisted. "Was that exercise helpful?" There was some nodding.

"It's a bit embarrassing," Ying said nervously. "I think I need to start again with my CV. I wouldn't want people filling in the gaps to imagine what I'm really like."

"Then it sounds like you're starting to see yourselves through my eyes," Rich said. "Until I meet you, all I have to go on is that piece of paper. In fairness, it's a really rubbish way to decide who's in and who isn't but it's what employers do."

He paused a moment. "At the end of the day, this course is good for me but hopefully it's good for you too. You'll leave knowing what all employers are looking for and how they judge you – fairly or unfairly. You can't change the way they think but you can prepare for it and try to change what they think *about you*. If you complete the programme, I'll try to find you more work – if you don't, come back when you're ready."

The room was silent. He figured it was time to make an exit and wished them all well. As he moved towards the door, he put a hand on Antonio's shoulder and said, "Good to see you, mon ami."

As the door closed, Cheryl returned to the exercise and explained how the scoring system is supposed to be used by all decent employers and that it usually works to find the best candidate.

She said that in the UK, it's what bosses use as evidence if they're ever accused of being prejudiced against someone.

"Woe betide any employer who cannot prove that they didn't turn someone down because they were not as good as the successful person. They can end up in serious trouble, costing the company dearly."

She explained they would come back to look at which groups were protected under law to prevent bosses treating them unfairly.

"How many of you were surprised how much you could tell from such short statements?"

Almost everyone put their hand up.

Ying hesitated, then opened her mouth to speak. "I'm not sure I'm happy with how much we read between the lines. We don't really know if Steve is a negative person or if Yusuf might not be happy with an admin job. It doesn't feel very scientific."

"That's life though, innit?" Naz replied. "We all assume stuff about other people. You'll assume things about me and I'm assuming things about you. All you can do is try to give a good impression and let them assume the right things about you."

"It's an art, not a science, like," Jock called out.

"Quite right," Cheryl said, turning to the flipchart. She began to write. After she was finished, she read the summary of Sign 1 out loud.

SIGN 1 – WHAT EMPLOYERS WANT

People who:
- Fit the job role on offer
- Can do the job safely and to targets
- Show they know what employers want

They wrapped up for a coffee break and Cheryl disappeared from the room. Naz and Jock were first to grab a hot drink and started talking in the corner near the biscuits. They were speaking quietly at first because the room was so quiet, with no-one else talking at all.

"Typical Rich to come and put a spanner in the works," Naz moaned.

"What do you mean? He was just saying 'hello.'"

"Nah. He was putting his imprint on things, making sure we hadn't forgotten who was in charge. It's classic."

Jock was not impressed. "You've got it wrong, bud."

"Rich is not interested in all this. He just wants to make a buck. No, he wants us to make him a buck." Naz was not going to budge. "Cheryl's cool, but..."

"This was all Rich's idea. Cheryl works for him. You

don't know him."

"And you do?"

"Actually, I do. I've known him years. We've got some water under the bridge."

"Mate, he's just running a business. He wants workers who play the game, so he can have an easy life and make some profit."

Ying had stayed out of the argument until now. She had been surprised to find the workshop so interesting. She was worried Naz's attitude would spoil things.

"I don't see what's wrong with that, Naz. What employer doesn't want a workforce that just turns up to do the work they're asked to do? Maybe that's the point of all this."

"I'm just saying he's no saint and it's not all about us," Naz replied. "I've nothing against him but I don't feel the need to be grateful to him."

"Has he asked you to say thanks?" Jock asked.

"And where does the money go?"

"For goodness' sake, Naz," Ying snapped. She was growing angry. "This is stupid. You bite the hand that feeds you – why turn on someone trying to help you?"

"But that's what I'm saying. He's not trying to help us out. He has his own thing going on and we're helping him out."

"It's not-for-profit, Naz, so any money they make here goes back into the business," Jock said. "But I do kind of agree that we're helping each other out. Rich has said so a number of times. He doesn't pretend. It is what it is."

"Okay, then."

"But it's not a bad thing. It's just business. You do something for me, I do something for you." Jock was annoyed with Naz's smug smile.

"And that's employment," Ying added.

"I still think he couldn't care less about us."

"You don't know that," said Ying.

"Actually, I know for a fact that that's not true," replied Jock. "It's just his job to be the boss. He'll come in here and be all 'bad cop' but that's just because he doesn't want to muddy the waters. He isn't a bloody support worker. He doesn't want to run a charity. He has to demand standards and he can't be seen as a soft touch. Cheryl is 'good cop' and Rich has to be the one who says, 'No, not good enough.'"

"Whatever, mate. I think you're deluded."

An unfamiliar voice joined the discussion.

"You don't like Richard?"

Naz, Jock and Ying all turned around with surprise. It was Antonio.

"No-one – no one – has paid me to work," he said. "They just see this." He waved his hand wildly around his face and down his body, pointing out his appearance. "Not Richard. He pays me. Now I pay him back with working hard."

The room fell silent. No-one knew what to do. Naz opened his mouth, about to respond, then closed it again and looked at the ground.

SIGN 2: PASSION

The three key questions

Ying gave each of the jobseekers a sheet of paper with three simple questions on it. Cheryl said they had 10 minutes to think about their answers.

The questions were so simple, they seemed pointless to Naz. He tutted and wrote things straight down without thinking about the questions properly.

Cheryl ignored his negative reaction, knowing that all would become clear.

The questions were:

- Outside work, what do you like to do?
- What have you done that you feel proudest about?
- What is the best job or role you've ever had?

Cheryl walked around the room, making herself

available if people wanted to ask questions. She nodded at Antonio, who had bought a belt for his oversized trousers in the two weeks since the last session.

Jock, Alison, Naz and Ying were sat pretty much in exactly the same positions as last time too. After 10 minutes, Cheryl returned to the front of the room.

"Now to find what job you want to set your sights upon, let's look at what gets you going. Who shall I ask first? I want to know what you love doing. What is *your* passion?"

She looked at Naz, who squirmed. "Don't even think of asking me first, Cheryl."

"Ah, Naz," she replied with mock disappointment. "C'mon now. You've put yourself forward as far as I'm concerned. You look like a bored teenager, slouching in your chair with your arms folded. As you get to know me, you'll know I'm not going to let you get away with that. Is that how you'd sit in an interview?"

Naz straightened up without thinking and smiled in spite of himself. "What? No. Ask someone else."

But Cheryl wrote *Naz* at the top of a fresh new sheet on the flipchart stand.

"Ah, man…" he whined.

Jock thought, *He's loving the attention.*

Naz glanced down at his paper, flicking the page as he peered down. "I'm not going to lie. What I put was 'nothing much.'"

Cheryl was ready for him. "Really? Imagine this is a two-day induction for a job you actually want. Is that what you'd say? How do you think that comes across?"

Someone muttered "idiot" under their breath. Cheryl did not challenge the comment. Naz picked up the paper, took another look at the questions, and looked up again. "Okay, it's not a good look. I get it."

"Doesn't worry me but as I'm talking to you, what *do* you like to do?"

"I s'pose it's about socialising a bit. I do a bit of volunteering. That's probably more like what you want to hear. I help with lunches for the Krishnas when they do outreach in town."

Cheryl asked him what he enjoyed about it and how he found it fulfilling.

"I feel like I'm giving something back. I like to know that people benefit from what I'm doing – they're not going hungry or rooting around in bins, which I hate to see. It's degrading."

"You shouldn't judge," Ying pointed out.

"Some people dinnae have the choice," Jock added.

Naz was a bit flustered. "You're getting me wrong. I wouldn't judge. I wouldn't be helping out with the Krishnas if I did. That's not who I am. I just meant no-one should have to."

"I can see that, Naz," Cheryl said. "It's interesting, though, isn't it? You have to choose your words carefully when it matters what people think. You do think it matters, right?"

Naz thought carefully. "I guess. I could be working with everyone here tomorrow. You want to get off on the right foot."

Naz described what he did with the Krishnas, handing out the food and chatting to people, and how he felt part of a team.

"I'm pretty good with people – I like that side. Other people don't speak, so they do the cooking. I'm out there trying to make people's days slightly better with a chat and some food. That's what…"

"You're an idiot," interrupted Ying.

Naz stopped mid-sentence and looked at Cheryl like she was a referee and he'd been fouled. But Ying continued.

"You put on such a front. No-one would know that's your passion. Are you ashamed? It's crazy. How you are and who you are seem totally different. Your eyes light up when you're talking about that but in an interview an employer would have given up on you by the time you sat down."

Naz squirmed inside. He didn't know whether to feel good or bad about what Ying was saying. Worse, she was right. This stranger who had no right to say what none of his friends would tell him. Worse still, Ying was still speaking.

"You're upside down – what you hide is what good people want to see. Is feeding the homeless the most rewarding thing you've done?"

Naz looked around the room and noticed Alison and Jock were listening carefully. Jock had a smile on his face. Even Antonio leant forward trying to follow the discussion. Cheryl was looking at Naz, expecting him to respond.

"Firstly, no, I'm not ashamed of what I do with the Krishnas. It's just something I do. I guess I'm quite a private person…"

"You shouldn't be that here," Ying said, but Cheryl raised a hand gently and encouraged Naz to continue.

"The most rewarding role I had was in prison. I trained up to be a volunteer counsellor. I helped people who were struggling to cope or who had mental health problems. To be fair, that was most people in there if they were actually honest about it."

He smiled.

"It was hard, though, you know. Everyone in those roles needed therapy themselves, just to deal with what they heard in that place."

The room was silent as a tomb.

"I don't think about the past very often. There were some tough times. One day, a guy came along and had managed to get himself a razor blade. He'd hid it in the collar bit of his sweatshirt and he pulled it out while we were talking. The screw couldn't see what he was holding but I could. I felt the colour drain out my face and, as you can see, that takes some doing."

He laughed and Jock sniggered out loud, thankful the tension had broken.

"He was going to do himself in," Naz continued. "He wanted me to know he was serious. I thought he was going to do it there and then. I was in serious need of a toilet break, I can tell you. I don't really remember what I said. I guess the training kicked in. Whatever I said, in the end, the guy handed over that blade. He broke down in tears – oh, and *then* the guard wanted to know what was going on. I hid the sharp, though. The guy was only a few weeks short of release and I don't think he'd have made it. But he did. I'd love to know how he's getting on."

While Naz was talking, Cheryl had written as fast as she could onto the flipchart. She had caught most of the key details as a brief reminder about his story.

"Thanks, Naz." She paused. "People, what do you make of that?"

"He's a different person," Jock offered. "Who knew?"

"I'm confused," Alison said honestly. "I thought we were here to find out how to get a job. I wouldn't tell anyone any of that in an interview, or even at work once I started."

Ying nodded. "I know what you mean, Ali. Cheryl? Where is this going? Are we just supposed to be getting to know each other?"

"No, this isn't a getting-to-know-you exercise. Well, it sort of is, but Ali you're absolutely right, this isn't a dry run for an interview question."

She grabbed a sheet of paper again and flipped it over with a struggle. At the top of the blank page, she wrote *Skills & Qualities*.

"People, we have some ideas about the kind of work that would make Naz want to jump out of bed in the morning, right?"

People nodded slowly.

Cheryl continued. "Naz, I want you to reflect on what you told us and what you now realise turns you on… well, you know what I mean. What would give you satisfaction? You know, starting with 'helping others.' Make sense? While you're doing that, I need another volunteer to tell us about their passions – the things that get them going."

Alison held her arm half up. She hadn't really spoken and she could see Cheryl was pleased to see her come forward. As all eyes turned to her, she looked at the floor.

"I'm not sure I'm getting this at all. I don't have anything like him to talk about. Nothing positive has happened to me – I left school with no qualifications and a drug addiction. I have nothing to put on a CV. I don't even have a permanent address, just a hostel for single mothers."

"Jeez, we're an employer's dream team, aren't we?" said Jock.

"Okay, thank you, Jock," said Cheryl. "Let's just remember how we all ended up here, shall we? We're not interested in perfect people. They can sort themselves out. We are much more interesting. And while we're on the subject, if someone asked me what my work passion is, I'd tell them about Naz, and you, Jock, and Ali – mentioning no names, of course."

She wrote Alison's name onto yet another page of

the flipchart.

"Right, Ali…"

"Sorry, Cheryl, can I ask…?" Ying interrupted. She looked Alison in the eye. "Can I just ask, you're not a user now, are you?"

Alison shook her head, shyly.

"And you have a kid?"

"A little girl. She's 4. A real handful."

"My god. You have so much to write down. Isn't your daughter the reason you get up in the morning? Isn't she everything to you?"

"Yeah. More than the world."

"And you're not on drugs? How hard was it to come off?"

"The hardest thing ever. They say childbirth is hard, and it is, but getting clean is in your head."

"Alison, you're kind of my hero. You must be organised, disciplined, responsible…"

"Woah, woah, woah," Cheryl called out. "You're jumping ahead, Ying. But she's absolutely right, Ali, there are some real clues there as to what makes you tick."

But Ali looked confused.

"No, I don't think so," she replied. "Those are all the reasons I haven't been able to find work. I can't take a job if I can't leave at the drop of a hat if my girl's ill. I just wouldn't. She has to come first. There just aren't jobs like that, let alone for an ex-junkie."

She paused, shaking her head.

"This is a waste of time."

"D'you know what, hold that thought, Ali. I'm going to call a coffee break but before we do, let's just recap."

She revealed a blank sheet of the flipchart, again reading out what she wrote, so everyone was clear.

SIGN 2 – PASSION

Work out what you're passionate about so you can:
- Identify some of the skills and qualities you have
- Tell employers about things that say a lot about you
- Narrow down the kind of jobs you want (and don't want)

I'M READY

SIGN 3: SKILLS

Know yourself

"Ying, what do we know about Naz so far? What gets him going?"

Naz folded his arms and looked around the room at his fellow jobseekers.

"I don't think this is right question, Cheryl," he said. "What do employers care?"

Jock and a couple of others straightened up in their chairs to see what might happen next.

Ying jumped in. "We know he likes charity work."

"Right. Naz," said Cheryl. "What is it about helping others that you like? There must be something about it. It wasn't a one-off. You keep going back to it. What is it that inspires you?"

"It's not so much what inspires me, it's what pisses me off… sorry, what really annoys me." He paused to think a second. "I walk down the street and I see people in doorways and I think, *this isn't good enough*.

"Or I pick up a paper and read about a kid with cancer who's fundraising for underprivileged children – money to send them off for a week surfing in Cornwall. It gets me and I think that, really, we're pretty lucky."

Ying was fidgeting in her seat. Cheryl nodded to her.

"Naz, why don't you see that that passion is exactly what an employer wants to hear. I'm sitting here wondering why on earth you are unemployed… apart from your attitude. I don't have anything like that to share at an interview."

"You think?" Cheryl said, turning over the page of the flipchart. She wrote *Ying* at the top.

"Yes," said Naz, grinning.

Cheryl looked at Ying, smiling. "You told me you love to read and study. What is it you love about that, Ying?"

"That will teach me to open my mouth, won't it?"

Ying thought for a short while and Cheryl stopped anyone jumping in until Ying started, slowly.

"I suppose it originally started with my parents. They had high hopes for me. My dad died and I went a bit off the rails. Now I wish I'd stuck at things. That would make my mum happy, and with my dad looking down… I also like the… what's the word, working on my own, in quiet and peace… solitude? Yes, solitude. But I wish I did charity work, now."

Cheryl explained that the questions helped reveal how everyone is different.

"There's nothing stopping you being inspired by each other but the point is you want to be real to employers. If you're talking about something you're passionate about, you won't feel nervous. You're in your comfort zone and that's where you want to be in an interview."

She explained that employers often ask people why they want the role on offer. She then nodded at Ying.

"Ying, you could say something like: *Because I'm someone who works well on their own and it's something my parents raised me to enjoy.*"

She turned to Naz. "What about you, Naz? *I have a strong sense of social justice and find motivation in making the world a better place*, or something like that."

The jobseekers were nodding slowly, seeing how the dots connected.

"It won't go on your CV but it sure as hell should appear, in some form or another, in your covering letter or email."

She warned everyone she was now going to go round the whole group, so they'd better start thinking about their answers. Jock quickly readied his pen, so he'd be prepared.

"Remember, you might want to use the answer when asked that question in interview – assuming, of course, it is the right job for you…"

She grinned, looking at Naz.

"Imagine Naz in a job interview for a bank."

Cheryl set the group off again to work on their own but crouched down beside Alison and talked her through the questions. Jock watched out the corner of his eye and noticed how Ali's face changed within a few minutes. She began to relax as she jotted down her ideas with Cheryl's help. Soon she had written more than Jock and he was interested to know what she'd added to her sheet.

The Fox and the Hedgehog

Cheryl put down the polystyrene cup of rubbish coffee.

"If I had to ask you whether you'd rather be a hedgehog or a fox, what would you tell me?"

People stared blankly back. The silence felt awkward but she let it continue, not knowing who would cave first. She thought it might be Jock. But then Naz opened his mouth to speak.

"It's the fox, innit? He's smart, works things out, has a game plan."

"You'd think, wouldn't you?" Cheryl noticed Antonio had his hand almost raised. "Oh, I always forget, do you know what I mean by hedgehog?"

He shook his head.

"I have a handout, hold on." She passed around a cartoon picture of a fox and hedgehog.

"Ah," Antonio whispered. "Hérisson." He smiled, nodding. Cheryl asked him which he'd rather be and as he tried to explain that maybe it would be a hedgehog, he laughed that he couldn't even say the word.

"Maybe I should just stick at the fox?"

Cheryl smiled. "The fox will try lots of things. That's what we imagine, right? Sometimes they catch the hen, sometimes they don't. But we know they're cunning and sly. Yes?"

The group nodded.

"But hedgehogs know just one thing: how to roll up in a ball and avoid capture. So, which would you rather be?"

"Sorry, Cheryl, I'd still want to be the fox," Naz insisted and most of the group nodded in agreement.

Only Jock, knowing things with Cheryl were never straightforward, said: "I'd be a hedgehog. Maybe it's better sometimes to be spiky?"

"What does the Job Centre tell you to be?"

"Definitely a fox," said Naz. Everyone agreed.

"Right. And where does that get you? Knocking on every door, applying for every job?"

There was a smattering of 'nowhere' responses but Jock went further: "Ending up feeling like crap and pretty much not wanting to go for any job."

"So, what if we tried the other approach and tried to be a bit more hedgehog? We don't need to be spiky but we do need to know what our One Big Thing is. Because the thing about hedgehogs is they're slow and goofy-looking but they're pretty successful all the time at not being eaten. They just roll into a ball, being prickly. The point is, they're successful all the time."

"Not when they cross the road," Naz joked and people laughed.

"Well, that's when they don't stick to what they know best," Cheryl countered.

She explained how the Hedgehog Concept was devised by Jim Collins, a business expert who had written a book called *Good to Great*.

"He applied the idea to big businesses and found it was the deciding factor between which ones started good and went on to be great and which ones failed. Jobseekers can be great too. And we start by finding your hedgehog. At Seven Signs training, we call your hedgehog your *One Big Thing*."

Your One Big Thing

Cheryl drew three interlocking circles and pointed to the space where the three overlapped. In it, she wrote *One Big Thing*.

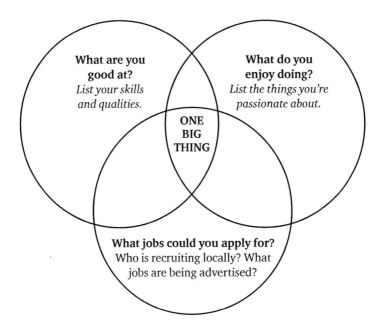

"So, how do we find your One Big Thing? We ask the same three questions we looked at earlier… and, guess what, you've answered one already."

The three questions:
- What do you love doing?
- What are you good at?
- And what jobs will pay you?

"Imagine having a job that pays you to do something you love and something you're good at. That's what we all should be working towards. We can feel confident we can succeed there. And each day we wake up, we'll be looking forward to being in work. It might not even feel like work. Think about that."

People started to grin. All except Naz.

"Yeah, right. Who has a job they look forward to doing?"

"Are you kidding?" Cheryl asked, smiling broadly, who right now was loving every minute of the job she was doing.

"Now we're going to look at those simple questions in detail."

Cheryl rolled back the flipchart paper to where she had listed the things Naz was passionate about. The group focused again, reminded of his belief in social justice, wanting to make a difference and reaching out to people in trouble.

"Okay, group, we learnt a hell of a lot about Naz with those three simple questions. He might not have meant to but he's given us enough to start reading between the lines about what he has to offer. What do you think? What words would you use to describe him?"

Cheryl had left plenty of room on the flipchart and she hovered over it with a different coloured marker pen.

"Ying, you had plenty to say about him."

"Well, he's charitable," she said, after a moment of reflection. "So, he's caring. He was fundraising. So, he's organised."

"Responsible," Jock added.

"Confident," Ying suggested, having considered and

rejected *arrogant.*

Within a few minutes, the list on the board read:

- Caring/compassionate
- Organised
- Responsible
- Confident
- Problem-solver
- Planning skills
- Uses own initiative
- Team player
- Communications
- People person
- Reliable
- Project management
- Leadership
- Hands on
- Inspiring
- Persistent
- Works to goals
- Fit

"So, for someone who likes to do nothing much, you seem to have quite a bit going for you."

Smiling, Cheryl continued. "Sorry, Naz, I couldn't resist that. But do you see why these simple questions open everything up? It's not rocket science."

Cheryl explained how, from here, Naz and all the other jobseekers would soon have a long list of skills and qualities that they could claim as their own. They would be unique to them too, not copied off a list in a run-of-the-mill CV-writing workshop. They would mean something.

Jock felt a little taller by the end of the session, feeling like he really did have something to offer.

"When it comes to listing skills on your CV," said Cheryl, "refer to this longlist and choose the five or six that are either your strongest or match the job you're going for best. Change them for each job, if you need to. And always, always, support them with examples of when you have used them, which is easy to do because they came out of what you have just told us all, about the things you have done already.

"This way an employer knows you're not just trying to sound good and they can ask you for more detail in interview, which by the way is a good reason not to have made stuff up on your CV. Be real. Be authentic.

"Ali, can we quickly run through your list?"

Cheryl explained to the group how Alison had agreed with Ying's suggestions and listed being a mother and getting clean of drugs as the things she was most proud of. Ali had told her that one of the things she felt strongly about was being the best mum she could be.

Then Cheryl asked the group to shout out the words they guessed would describe Ali. Before long, there was a longlist that Cheryl was pleased to see Ali was hurriedly writing down:

- Responsible
- Mature
- Organised
- Confident
- Flexible
- Role model
- Caring/compassionate
- Determined
- Disciplined/self-disciplined
- Good with children
- Aware of health and safety
- Supportive
- Positive
- Lived experience
- Hard working
- Motivated
- Persistent
- Patient
- Focused

When Cheryl asked Ali which of the long list of skills and qualities she saw in herself, she smiled broadly. She was surprised and not quite sure what to say. She kept re-reading the list.

"I'm pretty shocked. I don't know. I think I could give examples of when I've been all those things. Not sure I'm confident – I never feel that. But I could be the rest. Don't know what to say."

"Another satisfied customer, Cheryl," Ying called

out.

"All your work, guys. Ali, could you pick out the top five or six that describe you best. Maybe ones that you could give clear but quite different examples for?"

"Erm," Ali hesitated. "Determined and self-disciplined, obviously, coming off the gear. Maybe that's not a great example…"

"Well, it's a part of you," Cheryl offered. "It's something you are. I bet there are other examples of when you have been determined and self-disciplined."

Ali thought carefully and everyone stayed quiet. Even Ying resisted the temptation to chip in with suggestions.

"I really had to fight to get our place in the hostel. I might not tell an employer that. Well, I suppose I could tell them that I needed to arrange my housing for me and my girl and that I took advice and stood my ground. I really showed I knew my rights and what I was entitled to."

Cheryl was nodding.

"I think that's a pretty good example, especially if you have other things to talk about that could be a bit more about jobs. What else would be on your shortlist?"

"Organised – I do the admin for a voluntary group. It's Narcotics Anonymous but I wouldn't tell them that. Hard-working – well, anyone who's been a parent would get that, and being patient and responsible. Supportive – oh, I'm kind of mentoring a teenage mum who's struggling to cope. I'm helping her build bridges with her mother as there's a chance she'll take her back in. I'd quite like to do more of that, actually."

"Absolutely fantastic. I thought you said you had nothing to offer. Sorry, I'm not trying to catch you out but you know what I'm saying."

Cheryl turned to the flipchart. "Skills, then…"

SIGN 3 – SKILLS

Being clear about your skills means:
- Employers can see what you have to offer
- You can focus on finding work that you'll be good at (and succeed in)
- Your CV will be authentic, unique to you and supported with examples you can talk about

---

Breakthrough

"I wanted to show you something," Jock mumbled to Rich at the next of their catch-ups over coffee.

"What's that?"

"This. This." Jock pulled out a crumpled piece of paper from his pocket. It had originally been folded in four but since being stuffed in his pocket, it looked like an old tissue.

"What the hell's that? Origami?" Rich teased.

"No, man. It's my One Big Thing. The job goal Cheryl

helped us with. I think I've worked it out."

Jock tried his best to flatten out the little white sheet. He managed to push it into some coffee spilt on the wobbly table.

Rich laughed, swearing at him affectionately for being so clumsy. Then he took a look at the diagram on the paper.

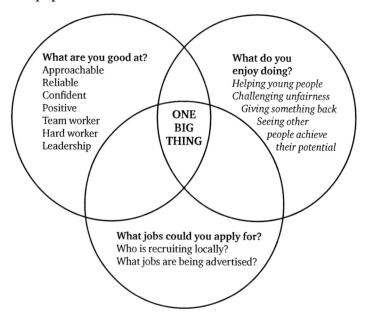

"Thing is," Jock said seriously, "I think it's time to get myself together because this totally feels like the right thing for me. Maybe not forever, but maybe it will be. But now I've got a goal. And I want this."

"Okay, okay, but what is it? Say it out loud, for goodness' sake."

"I want to work with kids. Ones who might be going the way I went. Not littl'uns, 14 or 15 year olds. I think back to me and I think it was really, really obvious I was going nowhere. You see here..."

He pointed to the circle with the things that he was passionate about and talked Rich through the background. He spoke with conviction.

"I believe you," said Rich. "And if you talk to them like that, there isn't an employer out there that wouldn't know you're serious about this kind of job."

Jock moved onto the circle with his skills and qualities in it.

"There are too many in here," he said. "I need to go through and shortlist the ones that I can talk about best and the ones that a youth homelessness or offender project might need. I know I need training but I've started looking at what courses are out there or what I could ask an employer for. I was thinking about looking for voluntary work, but..." He paused. "I'm going to need some help."

"With?"

"I got a record, man. And the drink."

"I won't lie to you, fella. It's going to be hard. You need to be realistic about your convictions. You're highly unlikely to find work with councils or in schools, for example. There will be other opportunities, maybe with charities who value your lived experience, so to speak – like we do.

"As for the drinking, you will have to be in recovery

and be able to reassure employers you have a strategy for any setbacks.

"Have you looked at what jobs are being advertised?"

Jock shook his head and said he'd only just hit on what he wanted to do.

Rich continued. "Well, then, let's see if we can fill out that third circle. It'll help us see what we're up against too."

They finished up their coffees, went back to Rich's office and turned on the computer. Rich loaded up Google and entered the words 'vacancies youth homelessness' into the search bar.

Jock's eyes glazed over. As far as he was concerned, this was all witchcraft.

"Jock, watch this. I'm not doing it for you in future so you'll need to learn. Ah, here we go…"

A list appeared on the screen with a number of websites. Some had specific vacancies, while some were recruitment pages with listings of multiple jobs on offer. Within half an hour, they had a list of the employers with jobs on offer in the city and what they needed from people wanting to work with young disadvantaged people.

They filled in the third circle on Jock's piece of paper.

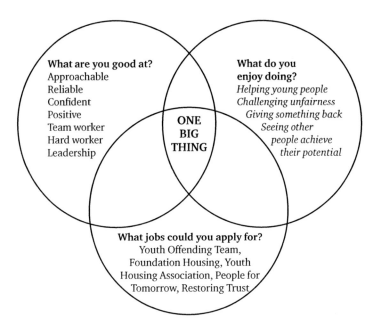

Rich smiled. "This is really coming along, Jock. Now of all the jobs in the third circle that are available, which ones could you apply for?"

Jock identified two that lined up with what he was good at (in circle one) and what he enjoyed doing (in circle two) and wrote them in the little space in the middle of the three circles.

"Jock, this is awesome. Don't you feel like you're getting yourself together? From the guy on the streets not able to see straight to someone who knows what they're about and where they're going. Fella, who wouldn't employ you? Maybe after a little brushing up on your job application skills."

Rich was genuinely happy for Jock and he knew it would not be long now until Jock was back in work and standing on his own two feet. He just needed a little more guidance from Cheryl and the right opportunity. But he was right on track.

SIGN 4: VISION

Looking to the future

It was the third session and Jock was thinking Alison seemed to have returned to her default setting of negative.

She seems to put all the barriers in front of herself, he thought. *It's hard enough finding the right jobs but if you can't even believe in yourself, or trust the people trying to help you, you've no hope.*

"I just don't think an employer wants to know that you have big plans for the future," she said. "They'll think you're full of yourself and that you already have one foot out the door before you've even been offered the job."

Alison was holding her own with Cheryl, arguing her point with confidence.

"What do the rest of you think?"

"Maybe it depends on the employer," Ying offered.

She didn't want to undermine Alison as they'd started to become friends but she still also respected Cheryl. "One might be impressed you are confident in yourself, another might find it challenging."

Naz felt he had something to say and was thinking hard about it. He could see both sides.

"I think Ying's right. To be fair, a manager for a massive chain like Starbucks or Marks & Spencer will like that you have something about you. I'm not sure that if you applied for a little shop or a local pub that they'd quite understand why you were telling them your big thing for the future. They'll probably secretly be hoping you're going to work for them forever."

A few of the group sniggered in approval.

"Probably on minimum wage too," he added.

"I think that's a fair comment," said Cheryl. "Thing is, a common question at interview is "Where do you see yourself in five years' time?" What are you going to say to that?"

"I hate that question," said Jock. "I never believe they care."

"Maybe not but what are you going to do, refuse to answer?" Cheryl was insistent. "Vision is one of the Seven Signs and although I think it's really important for you, if not for employers recruiting you, we only need to recap what we've covered already."

She flipped the paper on the stand to reveal a clean sheet and wrote 'VISION' at the top.

"Ying, tell me how we've looked at this already."

"Oh, erm, I guess, the… oh, yeah, the personal statements," Ying replied. "The person who got the job, er, Maria? She really knew what she wanted and for her, telling that to the right employer with the right job worked out. The guy who just wanted any job didn't do well at all."

"Perfect," Cheryl called out, writing down some key notes. "One place where you can show you have a vision for your own future is in your personal statement. And how might we get to the point where we know what to put into the statement?"

"Working out your One Big Thing?" Jock ventured.

"Your One Big Thing is absolutely your vision for the future. And how did we get there? Jock?"

"Asking what we're really into and what we're really good at – our skills and qualities. And researching the jobs we could go for."

"Exactly right. Blimey, I can't write fast enough."

"And hej-hock!"

"Antonio, you legend." Cheryl wrote *hedgehog* onto the sheet. "Darn right. Being focused on your One Big Thing means you're more likely to find the job that's right for you, even if it's a long way down the road and you have to take crappy, low-paid, stepping-stone jobs in the meantime. And that reminds me, what did we talk about at the start of the very first session?"

There was silence for a while. Cheryl finally caught up with her writing and turned to the group. Then she drew a funny-looking squiggle on the flipchart.

"This is a snake, by the way. No?" She waited. "Remember the board game and how we tame the snakes and build our own ladders? We can create our own luck by working to our strengths and narrowing our focus. Successful people often say they visualise where they want to end up before they start. What does that mean if it isn't about having vision?

"My vision for today was to get to this point where you all realise you know where you're going. Having vision is central to the Seven Signs, although they all overlap.

"Is this making sense, people?" Nods around the room. Cheryl turned to the flipchart and started to write...

SIGN 4 – VISION

A clear goal for the future is important because:
- It reflects your skills and interests. It's <u>your</u> One Big Thing
- All goals are motivating and the right goals give you confidence
- You show employers you're not just working for the money

Party time

"I want you to imagine you're organising a party," Cheryl announced. "Bear with me guys. You know there's a cunning plan in here somewhere. Settle down, grab your coffees. C'mon, Naz, sit your backside down.

"Right, you're organising a surprise party for a friend. It's their 30th birthday and, like most people leaving their twenties they're a bit fed up about it, but worse this friend is a bit of a control freak. Whatever you do, it's going to have to be good…

"So, I want you to list all the things you'll need to think about."

She gave them a few minutes, preparing the flipchart paper as she waited. As before, she guided them along like a shepherd and before long she had a list of all the things the group had decided needed to be organised:

- Venue [priority]
  - Research online for child-friendly ones
  - Visit three and select best
  - Must be completed at least three months before event (so invites can be sent)
- Date
- Guest list and contact details
- Theme – fancy dress?
- Decoration
- Drink
- Food

- Invitations
- Transport
- Local places to stay (for people travelling)
- Entertainment – live band or DJ
- Photographer
- Plot/ruse/lie (how will you get her to dress in keeping with the theme?)

They had also ranked them in order. They were clear which things needed sorting before anything else could be done and which ones could wait. For each point, they also had a number of tasks to perform, like researching online which venues were child-friendly and visiting the ones they shortlisted.

In turn, each of those had a deadline so it happened in good time before the event, like a countdown. The location had to be confirmed before invitations could go out, and they needed to go out early enough to help people keep the date free.

"We've talked about building our ladders... when you have a list like this one for planning a party, you can literally see how each step in turn takes you up towards the end goal in mind. The first rung on the ladder is researching venues online. Do you see?

"How many of you have seen jobs advertised in project management?" Cheryl saw Ying and Naz raise their hands.

"Well," said Cheryl, "all this is basic project management. But what you don't realise is you do it all the time. Ying, when do you do it?"

Even Ying, who always tried to offer something, was stumped.

"Okay, how about this," said Cheryl. "On my way home, I need to pick up some bits and pieces to feed my family tonight. Before I can do that, I need to check my bank balance and maybe transfer some money across."

A few people looked less puzzled. Cheryl saw Ying smile. "Do you see? My One Big Thing for this evening is to prevent a riot at home and make sure everyone gets fed. To do that, I need to cook. To do that, I need to shop. To do that, I need money in the right place."

"So now you're going to ask us to project plan our search for work?" said Naz.

"Yes. Actually, I want you to start thinking about the steps you need to take towards your One Big Thing. You'll list everything it's going to take, not starting with your dream job but your next job, which will be the first step towards your dream job."

"I don't follow," said Ying quietly. "Sorry, Cheryl."

"Well, let's work through an example," Cheryl said, looking around the room. "Would you mind, Ali? Where did you get to with your One Big Thing?"

"Well, I wasn't sure, but I think it was nursing. I have no idea where to start, though. But it ticked all the boxes – stuff I'm pretty good at and things I'm cool with, like looking after people."

"Excellent, Ali. That's brilliant. You pleased with that?"

"Well, it's a goal. I've got a lot to look into first."

"Sure," Cheryl agreed. "Guys, what's Ali's first step?"

"Take any job to get some money together," said Naz.

"Do you think?" She looked around the room. "Jock, do you agree?"

"No, I don't think so. She's got the Jobcentre on her back so she might not have any choice if she wants to avoid sanctions but if she did, say, have a choice between working in a shop or in an old people's home, maybe she should choose the care home. That's me. That's what I would do."

"Does that make sense?" Cheryl asked the group. "Once you've set your long-term goal, your One Big Thing, you can start to make smarter choices."

Naz grinned. "Yeah, but wiping old people's bums…"

"You should grow up, Naz," said Ying. "When you're a carer, or a mum, you just do that stuff. If Ali can't do that, maybe it's the best bit of research she'll do – realising nursing isn't for her. She could get training in the old people's home. You can really get on. Get your training and get out."

"Or stay," Cheryl said. "Some people are happy in regular, unglamorous jobs for years. But yes, if you've set yourself a goal and you're going for it, think about the stepping stones you can move between.

"Because you know you want to show the employer your passion, your motivation and your vision, you can ask about training at interview. And they can help you with care certificates, infection control, manual handling of people, whatever training they might have that will help you work towards your goals."

Alison was busy making notes. She felt quietly excited about the prospect of starting down the road towards nursing. It felt right, like a number of things were coming together for her.

She felt like it was the first time in her life when she'd actually had a goal, at least one that did not involve another fix or the next feed for her little girl.

Ali looked around the room and guessed most people there felt the same.

I'M READY

SIGN 5: ASKING FOR HELP

Bad weather, wrong clothes

Rain hammered on the four windows lining the long wall of the workshop room. The strip lights hummed and Cheryl was tempted to close the blinds. She noticed that the mood in the room seemed more gloomy, like the clouds had set in inside too. She suddenly shouted, "Okay, everyone, stop!"

Unplanned, she asked them to move to the part of the room nearest the signs *Agree* or *Disagree* depending on how much they identified with this statement:

There is no such thing as bad weather, just the wrong clothes for the weather.

Straight away, the group was shocked into action. They forgot about the actual grey skies and turned their minds to Cheryl's question. They moved around the room and ended up pretty well spread.

Naz surprised Cheryl by opening up without

prompting.

"This is a real state of mind question, Cheryl. Positive people will see the good in everything and stand one end…"

"I don't agree," Ying responded. "It's not about being positive, it's about taking responsibility. If people think they have control over their own lives, they won't blame the weather when they get soaked through to their underpants."

"What do you think, Ali?" Cheryl asked.

Alison was stood closest of all of them to the sign saying *Disagree.*

"I totally disagree. If it's raining, it's raining. There's no arguing with that. Bad weather is bad weather. If I'm cold, I'm cold. I can't change the weather. No-one can."

"In a way, you can't argue with that," replied Jock.

Cheryl brought everyone back to their seats in a circle in the middle of the room. They continued to discuss the question, each of them shifting a little closer to shared agreement, reflecting how they'd come to respect each other in spite of their differences.

Ying said that if you think harder about the statement, half of it is about the actual weather and half is about your response to it.

"I do get that you don't notice the bad weather if you're prepared for it," Alison conceded in the end.

Cheryl moved the conversation on. She asked what people felt about financial disasters like a car breakdown, a water leak, or being sanctioned and having benefits withdrawn. The group considered how having savings were the equivalent of carrying an umbrella in case of rain, although not everyone has the means to set money aside.

They reflected on how being poorer seemed to cost more and the injustice of that, and Cheryl jotted down the group's collective shortlist of steps that anyone could follow to weather a cash crisis or improve their own luck when the worst happened:

- Be disciplined: put a little cash away each week somewhere safe
- Keep to the Jobcentre's rules: show willing/keep trying and don't get sanctioned
- Buy bargains: make sure it's a good deal first (and save the extra cash)
- Only borrow in emergencies and always pay the full amount back as soon as possible
- If you're struggling, get help
- Write a budget and stick to it

"These small steps are great and each one takes you closer to being ready for any setbacks but why are we talking about this on a course about finding a job?" said Cheryl.

"Is it about creating your own luck again?" Ying ventured.

"Partly, but not totally." No-one offered any further

thoughts, so Cheryl continued. "It's about resilience."

She wrote the word on the flipchart and circled it.

"That is, it's about how we protect ourselves against setbacks. What kind of setbacks might you be afraid of?"

"Being turned down for a job."

"Exactly. That's a big one. It knocks your confidence."

"Relapse."

"Totally."

"Child's sick."

"Bereavement."

"Getting nicked."

"Falling into debt."

"Getting depressed."

"You guys are on it this morning," laughed Cheryl. "These examples are exactly what I'm talking about. They can happen to anyone anywhere but if you've been there before, and we know many of us in this room have, these things can be hanging over our heads the whole time. They can become barriers just out of fear, right? No-one else has to do or say anything, they're just there. So, what do we do about it?"

Alison raised her hand and started to speak. "On the 12-Step, they say you have to start by accepting you have a problem."

"Do you all agree?"

"Only that that's a good first step," Naz replied. "I'm not a big fan of the programme as a whole. It doesn't work for me, the whole idea of accepting there's a higher power. You have to take care of yourself."

"That's not what that means," Ali said.

Cheryl stepped in. "Let's not debate the 12-Step Programme. But you're raising some interesting points. What responsibility does the employer have for your wellbeing?"

"None," said Naz, and Ying agreed.

"You're both right," said Jock. "The boss needs workers who are fit to work. And they have a legal duty sometimes to help you if you're, say, disabled. But at the end of the day, he or she can't take care of everyone. You have to play your part."

"Okay," Cheryl interrupted. "So, let's look back at this list about protecting yourself against a cash crisis. Which of those do you think is the most important and could be applied in the context of work?"

"Show willing?" offered Naz.

"Asking for help," Jock said sadly.

"Why do you say it like that, Jock?"

"I've just realised something." He looked around the room. Everyone was looking at him, expecting him to say more. "But I can't talk about it now."

Ancient history?

Jock decided to use the 15 minute break to take himself off outside for a walk to clear his head. For once, it wasn't the drink clouding his mind. It was something Cheryl had said that had made him think back to his past. Things could so easily have been different and so many years had been lost.

Jock had been selling The Big Issue magazine for about three years when he was invited to start working with the company as a sales volunteer.

Other vendors were shocked at first and some asked if the company was joking about taking him on.

"Talk about poacher turned gamekeeper," one person grumbled.

He felt he had earnt that opportunity, though, and most people accepted that, even if they were a little jealous. It had brought out a big change in him: he was surprised by the difference. Most homeless people in Bristol had known him since he was a hard-drinking, drug-using rough sleeper.

He'd started in Scotland, moved along the traveller route and stopped off where life was laid-back and people found drugs easy to come by. He could have travelled on further to Bath, where the begging was good, or onto the ends of the line in Bournemouth or Plymouth, but in Bristol you could live under the radar, getting what you needed and surrounding yourself with like-minded people.

He was one of the first to start selling The Big Issue there. He made no bones about it – it was better than begging. And it turned out he was good at it. And that made him feel good. In less than a month, he couldn't imagine anything worse than going back to begging, where looking as miserable as possible won you the most handouts. When he started selling the magazine, he felt he could stand all day with his head held high, chatting with people who wished him well.

Jock became the most successful vendor in the city. He could buy decent food and some watertight footwear. Before long, he was embarrassed if one of his 'regulars' ever stopped to chat and he was slurring on cider, so pretty quickly it was off the menu for breakfast. Then lunch. He started thinking about the future and began to turn up at the night shelter, progressing soon to a hostel place, which meant he could keep his new kit safe and clean.

One customer, Laura, worked in the bank opposite his pitch. She met him around Christmas, about 18 months after he'd started. In December, sales of the magazine soared because passers-by shared a mixture of guilt and goodwill towards the homeless people who sold it, and Jock was earning more than the staff back at the office.

Jock could really turn on the charm through his strong Glaswegian brogue. He had a cheeky grin, a sparkle in his eye and the dirtiest laugh. Laura was smitten and, unable to believe his luck, Jock soon moved into her flat. She was never phased by his stories; how he'd been thrown out of home by his dad, how he'd been sleeping rough pretty much on and off since he was 15, how he'd arrived in Bristol five years earlier. He was 31 and, even then, looked nearer 50.

It wasn't long before his manager, Cara, and one of

the other directors who worked behind the scenes, Rich, noticed how Jock would take no nonsense and taught the other staff what was firm but fair. It was impossible for vendors to accuse him of not understanding what they were going through and, of course, they all looked up to him for both his ability to sell and for the transition he'd made from the streets to a home, a fiancée, and a job. By the following Easter, he was a keyholder for the office and working full-time with the company.

After-work drinks were always fun and Jock was able to let his hair down with his colleagues, never one to turn down a drink. There was nothing to tell him apart from anyone else who worked there. He was simply accepted as one of the team. But he had an eye for the ladies and once or twice he hadn't made it home.

As Jock stood outside in the car park, drinking his lukewarm coffee, the memory of those nights filled him with shame.

As the reality of a settled life with Laura took hold he had begun to grow frustrated. He lobbied for more responsibility at work and grew annoyed that he seemed locked into the position he'd been in for months. Looking back now, he could see he had wanted too much too soon and never stopped to appreciate everything he had achieved.

Laura kicked Jock out the following summer and a few weeks later magazine vendors arrived at the office to pick up their copies and found it still locked. Cara was called in from her day off at 11.30. No Jock. No laptop.

No week's takings in the safe, either.

Cara was devastated. She left the company six months later to work for a corporate firm. Rich spent the next five years refusing to apportion blame and determined to make something positive of the whole affair. Eventually he moved on from The Big Issue.

Today, it was a lot for Jock to cope with, now he was in a place where he could look at the past with clarity. He felt a deep sense of regret, not only for what had happened but also for blocking it out with drink and blame… blaming the company for letting him fail.

Now everything had changed. It was time for him to take responsibility but it was a lot to take on. Rich did not want to talk about the past. Was this his way of punishing Jock?

"No," Jock said out loud. "I made lots of mistakes but one big one. I should have asked for help."

He wandered on back towards the training room. *Yes,* he thought, *things got out of control but I just should have held up my hand and said 'stop.' That was my mistake. One I won't make again.*

Time to come clean

Jock was sure about this one and held his arm full in the air. Only two other people did the same and they did not seem as certain as he was. At least Cheryl hadn't asked them to move around the room this time.

"Okay, so, you three disagree. The rest of you agree that it's important you discuss your problems openly with your employer? Okay, Naz, you agree with the statement?"

Naz nodded. "To be fair, it seems like you wouldn't ask the question if you didn't think it was important. It seemed like the right answer. But I think I agree, because it's about trust. The boss needs to know what's going on with you so he can trust you and you need to be able to trust him…"

"Or her," Ying chipped in.

"Or her." Naz smiled. "You gotta be open."

Cheryl turned to Alison, who was trying too hard to avoid making eye contact with her.

"Do you agree with Naz?"

Ali blushed, opened her mouth to speak, but couldn't think of exactly what to say.

"Is it important to have trust, Ali?"

"I guess."

"It is, isn't it?"

Cheryl shifted her stance, looking around the room. But again she spoke directly to Ali.

"Is it always right to share everything with your employer? Let's break it down again. Are there some things you might tell HR and some things you might tell your supervisor and other things you would never tell the big boss?"

"I guess. Yeah. I'd need someone to know if my kid was ill but I don't think a director would be interested, they'd just want to know I can do the job. Someone in personnel might be more understanding. My supervisor would need to know but only if it was likely I might have to leave early. So they can work around it."

Naz put his hand up. "What if you had a court appearance and you might go down? It might be an idea to tell someone in HR, in confidence, like. It might never happen. You'd still need time off as you gotta appear, but you might not go down."

Cheryl said this was a thought-provoking example with an encouraging smile. To avoid other people taking issue with the general point, she turned to Jock. He jumped in before she could say anything.

"Well, I'm a drinker and I wouldn't want anyone at work to know." He waited. Nobody laughed. Everyone was listening.

He went on. "I don't want anyone to think I would let them down. No-one. The boss. HR. My colleagues, y'know."

"I think that's really brave," said Ying. "To tell us. I wouldn't have guessed."

"I think I told you all in our very first session."

"That seems so long ago. Just goes to show that first impressions can be changed once you get to know people."

"I guess. I'm dry when I'm working and this is kind of like working. So drink doesn't even cross my mind… well, a bit."

Everyone was either looking at him or at Cheryl, to

see what she might say, but she said nothing. Jock had the floor.

"And d'you know something else? This is the only company recently that has taken a chance with me, and even if it's only been a bit of work here and there, I haven't let them down. I just wouldn't mess this up."

Cheryl raised herself up to speak.

"Ying's right, Jock. It's great that you're that open with us. The irony is that we *are* your colleagues. What do you all make of that?"

Naz started. "Yeah, I think it's cool. You said you didn't want to let your colleagues think you might let them down but you told us. It comes back to what I said. It's about trust. For me, it's easier to trust you because you came clean."

This made Jock think. He still felt he would rather not tell people.

"You have to decide what's right in the workplace you're in," said Ying. "You feel safe here. That's good." She smiled. Jock decided he liked Ying.

"Again, it's a good point," said Cheryl. "How would you all feel if Jock was having a bad day, though?"

"It's easy to jump to conclusions," Naz offered. "If he was late back from lunch by ten minutes. Maybe he'd got himself locked in the bogs. I might assume he'd fallen off the wagon. I'd start to get pissed off."

"We gotta look out for each other," said Ying.

"Yeah, but there are limits," countered Naz. "You can't carry people."

Jock shook his head.

"And that's why I shouldn't have told you. I'm an idiot." Then he laughed, seeing the funny side.

"Okay, so what does the employer care?" Cheryl asked, bringing the group round to the point of the discussion. There was a short silence.

"He – or she – doesn't care," said Naz. "Well, they might care but they just want the job done."

"Exactly!" Cheryl exclaimed. "They might care but they have a job to do and what matters is that you get *your* job done. They need to know you are earning your money safely and productively and no-one else feels they're carrying you. When is it vital you disclose any problems you're having, Naz?"

"If you're having a wobble?"

"That's probably as good a way as any to say it. Everyone, *everyone*, has wobbles. Of the millions of workers in this country who have never been homeless, or in prison, or unemployed for any length of time, absolutely any one of them can lose a relative, fall into debt or have an accident. Any one of them can become mentally ill, resort to petty crime…"

"Or be an alcoholic," chipped in Naz.

"Absolutely, or drink too much. The point is that an employer may or may not care about the issue but they definitely will care if it affects your work. Whose responsibility is it?"

Jock stepped up. "Mine. Ours. If we have a problem, own it. Don't let it become the employer's. That's when it's all going to go wrong."

"Damn straight," Naz shouted.

"Quite," said Cheryl. "Good employers – but let's face it, not all employers – will be flexible and offer to make what's called 'reasonable adjustments' if they can. They might give you compassionate leave or flexible hours, if you need to literally work around counselling or appointments, but they cannot run the business around you. There will be a limit. But it's down to you to ask for help when you need it."

After a pause, Ying offered: "It's not enough just to ask for help, though, Cheryl. You have to take it. You might say you're depressed but there's nothing your manager can do about it. They can give you time off but you have to do what you can to find help to get better."

"Exactly right. It's a fair deal, isn't it?"

Everyone nodded thoughtfully.

"How many of you have ever NOT applied for a job because you thought you'd have to either hide a problem or tell your employer you have one?"

Each person in the group put their hand up.

"I'm not going to embarrass you by asking but I hope you all feel slightly more confident that there are ways to manage these things. It's a grey area. Just ask for help when you need it."

"Or you'll be out on your arse!"

"Or you'll be out on your *ear*, Naz," Cheryl laughed. "And that's because there isn't anywhere for an employer to go if you let them down without a good explanation or without a commitment to sort things out, if you can."

Cheryl was really pleased with progress. There was one more area she needed to cover.

"When must you absolutely disclose a problem?"

Blank faces. "So," she explained, "by 'disclose' I mean in the legal sense…"

"Ah, if you've been nicked," Naz offered. "You know, if you have a criminal record."

"Not any criminal record, though," Ying said. "Not sure what the rules are."

Cheryl explained how it often depends on the nature of the offences on a criminal record and on the type of job the candidate is applying for.

"It's always best to get advice. I think a lot of people assume they will be asked to declare everything on their criminal record but many, many employers just don't check, so why worry them?"

She continued. "If the job is working with children or vulnerable people, they will definitely DBS check you anyway, so there's no point hiding it."

"What's DBS?" Ying asked. Cheryl threw the question open to the group and Naz correctly explained it was the Disclosure and Barring System, where all criminal record information is kept.

"So, what would *I* do?" said Jock. "My sheet just has petty offences on it. Lots of them, mind."

Cheryl looked thoughtful.

"Well, let's not go into the nitty gritty here but my

advice would be that if you're applying to work in a shop or a restaurant kitchen, you might not tell them unless you're going to be checked anyway.

"If you're working somewhere else, any convictions for petty crime more than a few years old might be considered 'spent,' in which case you can choose not to disclose but any more serious crimes, especially violent or sexual ones, will always come up.

"Now, in those cases, it pays to have a damn good explanation and some sort of reassurance that it's in the past and won't happen again. For some jobs, though – and this is the kicker – it will automatically disqualify you."

"What about my personal statement, Cheryl?" Jock asked. "I've tried to make a positive out of something and said I'd use that negative experience to help others."

"I think that's a great strategy, Jock. Just don't assume all employers will be looking for that."

She paused. Then asked the group in general: "Picking on Jock for a little longer, given what he disclosed to us earlier, when else *must* you come clean with the boss?"

"I'm not sure he must tell them he's had a problem with drink," Ying said protectively.

"What, never?" Cheryl responded. There was quiet. "What about if I asked him to take a shift on a bar at an event we were running?"

"I still don't think he needs to disclose," Naz chimed

in. "But he should make his excuses and turn the work down."

"Okay, fair point. Let's take a different example. What about if someone had something like diabetes?"

No-one had a ready answer.

"This actually happened. We sent a guy out to deliver leaflets for us and he turned up with no lunch and no money to buy food. After a few hours in the sun, posting leaflets through letterboxes, he keeled over. It was only then that he told his team leader he was diabetic. He was on the verge of going into a coma. Luckily, the team leader had a few quid on him to get him a sandwich and a chocolate bar but that could have been a disaster."

"Yeah, he should have told you," Ying said. "You could have worked round that."

"Dead right," Cheryl retorted. "We employed him again after that but only on the basis that he had a snack and money for food in future. He was over the moon. It turned out he'd not been applying for jobs because he was scared it would count against him. Now he knows that he just needs to say."

Jock asked when the right time would be to declare a health problem. Cheryl described how employment law in the UK means candidates should no longer be asked about their health conditions during the recruitment process. It should only come up once the job has been offered and, unless it means the individual just cannot do the job, it should never affect the decision.

"Before we move on," Cheryl said, "just remember

that if there's anything in your background that means you cannot do a certain job, make sure it is ruled out of your *One Big Thing.*

"For example, if you've been convicted of a violent or sexual offence and want to be a teacher in a school, I'm sorry but it's just never going to happen. I know I've asked you to focus on what you're passionate about and what you're good at but, honestly, there are some facts of life that might just limit those options, especially if the law is involved.

"So," she said, smiling. "Face up to them now and hone in on something you can achieve over time."

Cheryl took out the thick black marker once more, reading what she wrote aloud.

SIGN 5 – ASKING FOR HELP

Having a strategy around asking for help will:
- Prepare you for any setbacks
- Clarify when it's right to tell your employer you're struggling
- Leave your boss to just worry about you getting the job done

---

You're the boss

"I'd tell her she stinks."

"No, Naz, you wouldn't," said Ying. "It would be like telling your mum. It would be totally different in that situation for real. It's easy to be hard-line here."

Cheryl let the group continue to argue. The comments came in thick and fast.

"You'd definitely need to tell her but you'd have to be sensitive. The scenario on Cheryl's handout says Sheila's been with the company for years. She'll have loads of experience. We'd have to respect that and we'd want to keep her."

"But you can't have someone with bad body odour on reception. It's bad for business. Customers will walk away - they'll think we all smell bad. It's our reputation."

"It's not just bad for our business. It's not good for her either. It says here people have been laughing about her. What if she heard that? That might be worse than me telling her she stinks."

"There is that."

"She might have problems. Maybe her bathroom's out of action."

"She should tell someone. Get some help."

"Maybe there's a shower she could use at work."

"Or she could be taken off reception until her bathroom's fixed."

"It might not be that. She might have a medical problem. We'd need to ask her. Sensitively."

The conversation continued and the group reached a consensus around how they would help Sheila, the woman depicted in the scenario. Cheryl began to round up the discussion in preparation for the next.

"Okay, guys," she said. "This session is called *You're the boss* and look at you, all managers and supervisors in the making. It's not rocket science but it takes some thinking about.

"And you're absolutely right. Sheila deserves respect and sensitivity but your business requires you to do something about her personal hygiene. It's hugely personal but, as the manager, it's your job, so you have to do all you can to show it's nothing personal against her. Very tricky. Personally, I'd take her for a coffee and a chat. Maybe I'd be the first person she opens up to. But that's not everyone's style."

Cheryl then passed around the next scenario for them to consider.

SCENARIO TWO

Marius is a committed Christian with deep-rooted faith. Yesterday, a younger woman named Silvia was in tears in your office because Marius had commented on what she was wearing, saying it was "asking for trouble." While she was talking to you, she also said he had made comments about colleagues of different faiths, calling them names and being disrespectful. Silvia said she is not the first person to get upset, just the first person to report it.

You are the manager of a team. Problem-solving is part of the job and sometimes people have forgotten what's expected of them. You have to put things right but in the right way. This is a highly sensitive subject but one that cannot be ignored.

- What are the risks if you don't handle this right?
- Marius is scheduled for a meeting with you in half an hour. How will you deal with this?

There was a short silence as people read the scenario. Then they discussed it out loud. Cheryl could spot the natural leaders. Jock would let someone make a point but then lead the discussion. She gave them five minutes, then took her place near the flipchart.

"With Sheila and her body odour, and most of these scenarios, there is not so much right or wrong, it's more about achieving the best outcome for all concerned using whatever style you're most comfortable with." There was total silence. "But not with Marius and Silvia. The full weight of employment law is on your shoulders here."

Cheryl explained how certain groups were protected against unfair practice in the workplace. She kept the language simple and clear. The group was well-engaged anyway but she continued to ask questions, crediting them with a good sense of how the system would work and how the threat of tribunals hangs over the heads of employers.

"Complying with the law falls to everyone but discretion is taken out of managers' hands on these matters. With this particular example, it is difficult to know who is right and wrong but you must take action and be seen to take action, otherwise both Marius and Silvia may have a legal case against you.

"Marius could accuse you and the organisation of prejudice on the grounds of race or faith, as could Silvia because of her sex. In the UK, there are nine protected groups. I've just mentioned three. What are the other six?"

Soon, Cheryl had them all listed on the whiteboard:

- Race

- Faith
- Sex
- Age
- Disability
- Sexuality
- Parental status
- Marital status
- Transgender status

"It is simply illegal to make decisions based on these factors."

"But young people do often have a bad attitude," Naz argued.

"And older people," Alison countered.

"And you could both end up in court saying things like that," Cheryl pointed out. "And it's not just with existing employees you have to be careful. It's the same with recruitment. You can choose not to recruit people who seem to have a bad attitude but you can't say it's because of their age – and you need to be able to prove they seemed to have a bad attitude.

"I once heard someone say that young people had unrealistic expectations. Of course they do and that's down to a lack of experience but if you're their manager, it reflects on you if you don't show them the way. Good on them if they sue you for treating them badly."

She continued. "Same goes for speaking English or needing a woman, say, for certain jobs; you have to be able to prove the job has to be done a certain way. You can't just turn down someone based on their race, if English is a second language, or because they're a man or transgender."

"Shame ex-offenders aren't on that protected list," said Jock.

"Or homeless people," added Naz.

The group worked through three more scenarios by lunchtime. One looked at boundaries and the blurred lines between being friends and colleagues, another at attitude and poor performance, while the last one focused on health and safety.

Cheryl was struck by how passionate people were about the discussion. You didn't see this in the Job Centre. The jobseekers here cared about stuff. They felt it mattered.

"I'm paranoid I smell," Jock said quietly to Ying, who reassured him.

"It's funny, though," he continued. "I get how it's important to ask for help but sometimes you don't know you need help. You're at the mercy of others telling you and if they don't… what then?"

Ying bit her lip. "I don't know. Maybe we have to make sure there are people around us we trust to tell us. Maybe that's inside or outside of work."

Jock turns a corner

Jock noticed Rich kept looking at him suddenly, then looking away. They were in a coffee shop in the centre of Bristol. From their table, Jock could see the spot that used to be his begging pitch.

"Jock," Rich burst out eventually, "there's something different. What is it?"

"Ha ha. You noticed."

"Yeah, but noticed what?"

"New jacket?"

"Oh my god, Jock. Not just a new jacket – a suit jacket. And jeans that don't have your undercarriage all hanging out. Jeez." Rich leant back to peer under the table. "And shoes, you're wearing shoes."

"I've been setting some wages aside. Put 20 quid away each week for the past two months. Blew it on the clobber. You impressed?"

"Actually, I really... Jock, you've had a haircut!" Rich giggled loudly and grinned. "Mate, you look the business. I bet you were crying in the barbers, losing those dreads."

Jock laughed. "Aye. They hurt as they amputated them."

"No anaesthetic?"

Jock's playful sense of humour had always shone through the street-ingrained dirt and what used to be his dishevelled demeanour. He couldn't help but grin.

Rich was laughing as well. "I'm such a dumbass. That's brilliant. My friend, you're on the up. Seriously. You've got your One Big Thing, new clothes, a haircut. Oh, and is it true you've moved into a hostel?"

"Aye," said Jock, immensely proud of himself. "It's

true."

"That's great, Jock. Really. It's all coming together for you."

"That used to be my pitch out there. You couldda just walked on past. I'd still be out there today. Or I might have drunk myself to death by now."

"Mate…"

"Thanks, though."

"Not this again. Jock, you would have picked yourself up eventually. You had it in yourself the whole time. You know you did."

Jock smiled, not sure if he believed Rich, but then looked away awkwardly. He was thinking of when they had worked together before. Of Laura, his ex. Of how he'd let Rich down.

"Rich, I…"

"Water under the bridge, Jock. Time to look to the future. For both of us."

Jock's throat dried up.

Rich smiled. "One more session to go, fella. Cheryl says she wants you there early to go through your CV."

"No worries. I'm looking forward to it."

SIGN 6: PRESENTATION

Creating your elevator pitch

Cheryl could not delay the start of the session any longer. It was unusual for Jock to be late, but she had to think about the group, so she decided to crack on.

As she tuned into what was going on around the room, she noticed Naz and Ying chatting to Ali about two job ads she'd printed out for bank work at a children's centre where she hoped she could get some training and experience during school hours.

Cheryl thought it might be the first time she'd seen Alison really smiling. The other two were trying to encourage her and sharing their ideas about how she might want to specialise in nursing kids in the long-term and could do worse than start by asking Rich if there was any peer support work going.

Cheryl looked at the clock above the door one more time and called the group to order.

"Okay, so today is the last session and in a way – actually, in every way – the past six weeks have all been leading to this. We've covered five of the Seven Signs so far and today we're going to finish off with your mouth and your feet."

"Weird," Naz said.

"That's you, Naz," Ying laughed. "You always have your foot in your mouth."

Cheryl continued. "All will become clear. Now, what was the exercise we did for the first sign we looked at? In our very first session. After the snakes and ladders. Anyone?"

Ali flicked through her notes. "What employers want."

"Oh, we did the recruitment panel thing," Ying added.

"Exactly right, guys. You looked at yourselves through employers' eyes back then but today we're going to revisit it as jobseekers.

"This session is all about *Presentation*," she said, writing the word at the top of a fresh flipchart sheet.

"After all, what's the point of planning all this if you don't know how to present everything you have to offer to an employer whenever the opportunity comes up? You all have so much to offer. It sounds cheesy but I've found you all genuinely inspiring but, and here's the thing, employers don't have six weeks to find out what you have to offer.

"So, we're going to work on your advertising, starting

with your personal ad. How would you describe yourself to an employer, if you had just 30 seconds? Anyone?"

There were no volunteers.

"Remember the recruitment panel exercise then? Well, here we're going to start work on your own personal statement."

Cheryl described how the statements she was looking for would read like little 'lonely heart' ads in the classifieds section of newspapers. But instead of wanting to meet the perfect partner, these ads want to meet the perfect boss.

"They will demonstrate clear vision. This means you will present the key skills and qualities you've already identified and the end job goal you're working towards."

"Is this what people call an elevator pitch?" said Ying.

Cheryl agreed it was and asked Ying to explain more.

"Well, I think the idea is that you step into a lift and by chance there's someone there who might have a job you're looking for. You only have a few floors before they'll get out the lift and you'll never see them again. You have to impress them before they disappear."

"Exactly right." Cheryl smiled. "It might not be literally in a lift but it could be in a coffee shop or bar, or in the street. You never know when something could come up in conversation. I've just done it myself. I bumped into the woman who runs this centre downstairs and she said she's looking for a tutor to run a workshop on starting your own business. I only had a minute before I came up here but, let's think, what did I say? It was something like…

"I'm just finishing training a group of fantastic jobseekers." Cheryl paused and grinned. "I'll be looking for some freelance training work, if you're looking for someone who can work with people who maybe need some inspiration and direction. I have a course I can adapt or work equally well delivering something you've put together already. I'm trying to get my hours to full-time, so I'd be really interested.

"I asked her if she wanted to meet and we're getting together next Monday. The point here is that sometimes you have a limited time and a unique opportunity to put yourself out there."

Cheryl flipped back a sheet of the large paper on the stand and revealed:

**As someone with [x, y, z skills/qualities],
I am seeking [first step job opportunity] to develop
my skills and experience, working towards
[my One Big Thing/long-term job goal].**

She continued to explain.

"There are lots of ways to write a personal statement. You've seen three already when we looked at who to employ for the admin job. But this template might help you get started, so you have something at least to show for today."

She set them to work, offering them just 15 minutes to see what they could achieve.

Naz stared hard at the words. He really didn't know where to start. After lots of scribbling, crossing out, and re-writing, he came up with:

As someone focused on a positive future and helping to create a better world, I want to put my people skills to use in a job where I can solve problems and offer some leadership in a management-level role. I am currently looking to take up a communications position for a campaigning charity where I can channel my commitment to social justice.

Ying begged Naz to show her what he'd come up with. He didn't want to but after she'd nagged for what felt like half an hour, he relented and passed over the untidy sheet of paper.

"My goodness. Naz, help me do mine. I can't do it."

Before long, Cheryl gathered the group back together whether they had finished or not. She asked Naz, and then Ali, to read their statements aloud.

"It kind of wrote itself once I had the template," Alison explained.

I am a committed and motivated individual with skills from being a parent working towards a career in nursing, possibly in children's health. I am currently looking for a role in the care sector where I can develop my skills and experience.

"Brilliant work," said Cheryl. "So good."

"That's amazing, Ali," Ying echoed.

"There's one thing I'd suggest you change, though,"

Cheryl observed. "You remember we said employers are not allowed to treat you differently if you're from one of those nine protected groups? Well, I wouldn't risk it and wouldn't mention you're a mum. Just like you wouldn't include your age or nationality on a CV."

"Yeah, it's not relevant here," said Naz. "What matters is you have the skills, not that you have them because you have a kid."

"Yeah, yeah, I forgot."

Ali crossed through a couple of words and added some more. She was so pleased, she was itching to get it typed up and added onto her CV.

"Right, so, we have plenty more to do on this but so I don't forget at the end of the workshop, let's just write up what we're talking about today..."

SIGN 6 – PRESENTATION

Presentation is all about being able to say that you're ready:
- You know how to tell an employer about what you have to offer
- Everything else grows from a personal statement
- It's like advertising – in the street, on paper, in a CV, or at interview

---

Do you have Clear Vision?

There was still no sign of Jock. Cheryl decided to get the group started and then pop to the office and try to call him. She was sure he would have a good reason.

In the room, everyone was so positive today. She had just asked how many of them had a CV already and about half the jobseekers had a hand in the air.

"And how many of you have brought your CV with you?"

A couple of hands came down.

"And how many would be willing to show us?"

No-one.

"So not one person has a CV they would show to a stranger? What does that tell me? Naz, what's so wrong with your CV that you can't show me? Don't worry, I'm not going to ask you to share it with everyone – we can go through it later, if you want to."

Confident as he was, he remained hunched forward on the uncomfortable plastic chair, staring down at a slightly creased set of papers.

"It's got everything I need in there. My life on two pages. There's loads of help for people wanting to put their CV together."

"Good," Cheryl replied. "So it has, what, a list of your skills? Your job history? Your interests?"

"Yep, all of that. I'm happy with it."

Frustrated, Ying called out: "So how come you're here, then?"

Naz looked around to see what he'd said wrong.

"I don't want to sound harsh," continued Ying, "but if your CV is that good, surely you'd be employed by now. Don't get me wrong. I'm not in a place to judge."

"Maybe he thinks the CV is a good reflection of him but that that's the problem," said Ali.

It was suddenly very quiet.

"I didn't mean that to sound like a dig, Naz," Ali added. "Sorry. You know what I mean."

Cheryl observed the group dynamic and the influence of peers on each other. She would never have challenged Naz like that but his friends had made a good point.

"Okay, so there's something here to chew over. Seven Signs training is partly about recognising that however good your approach has been so far, it hasn't worked yet. Maybe there's nothing to lose by trying something new.

"The thing about CVs, for me, is that they might work for you but if they don't work for employers… well, they just don't work. Why might I say to you that a CV is the last thing you need?"

Naz jumped in sarcastically. "Cos we've got one already?"

"Well, *you* might have," Ying retorted. "I was actually hoping to work on mine."

"Do you ever think you're being too honest?" Cheryl asked.

There was a brief discussion and agreement that it

was a bad idea to lie on your CV or at interview.

"I'm not suggesting lying," said Cheryl, "but maybe you're not seeing things through the employer's lens. Think about it. What does the employer need to know? Surely, it's just what you have to offer now and where you're going in future?"

There were murmurs of agreement.

"I want to reclaim CV to mean Clear Vision. Surely what matters is what you can do, and how willing you are to do it, not where you've been. I can tell you now that if your CV has a list of the jobs you've had in the past, what most employers do is look at how long you stayed in each one and how many gaps there are. We've had people on Seven Signs training that have been on the streets, been off sick for years or been in jail. Nothing spooks a new boss more than someone who looks like a bad risk."

Ying was nodding. "I think that's what's wrong with mine. It's all about the past. And the jobs I've had have been crappy part-time jobs that don't say anything about what I want to do in future. In fact they all only lasted a few months at the most and then nothing for the past 18 months."

"It's not going to work, is it?" said Cheryl. "What about your skills? How many of you with CVs have 'good communication' on the list?"

All those who had said they had a CV raised their hand.

"What about 'good with IT?'"

Most of the same people raised their hand.

"I hate to say it but a lot of CV-writing courses are like sausage factories and all your CVs come out looking the same. As an employer, I wouldn't be able to tell one person from the next. How many of you list examples of when you've used those skills?"

No-one raised their hand.

"Anyone can claim to have any skills but if you back them up with a short description of when you used them, it's harder to doubt them, isn't it? Ying, you had your hand up before. Give me an example of using your IT skills."

"Erm, on Facebook and Twitter?" She paused, awaiting approval or encouragement. Feeling awkward in the silence, she added: "I send a lot of emails. I did some research for a job I applied for by looking at a few of their ads on YouTube...."

"Right, so if your CV said 'good IT skills, used in research and communications,' does that sound better?"

Everyone nodded.

"If you do your CV right, it will be unique to you and that means it won't look like somebody else's. I can look round the room right now and tell you for a fact that no two people here are the same. I think you're all capable but some of you are better at some things and others will be better at different things. As an employer, that's what I really need to know. Not how many times you've been out of work in the past few years."

Naz raised his hand. "I can see where this is going. It's good. I'm starting to think of some ideas for brushing up what I've started but if I take out my work history, I won't have much left."

"Hey, it's *your* CV," said Cheryl, "which means you can do what you want but I think a decent CV can go on a single page – two at most. Your work history does not need to list every job you've had since the paper round you had when you were 13. It mainly needs to back up the claims you've made about the skills you have.

"Remember, 'Clear Vision' is about what you have to offer now and where you're going in the future. What difference does it make if you worked in an ice cream parlour one summer if you're now applying for a gardening job? If it's a customer service role, then that's a different matter. I'd summarise the jobs where I used the skills needed for the job I'm going for now. Does that make sense?

"And I'd re-read and, if necessary, re-write my CV before attaching it to each job application I make. It has to be unique to me but tailored for the employer. Do you see?"

There were a lot of people smiling and, Cheryl noted, writing ideas down.

"So why haven't we helped you with your CV on Seven Signs training yet?"

"Because we need to know what to put in it first?" suggested Ying.

"Exactly. Most of you just hadn't thought about all

you had to say until I started putting you through your paces. And you hadn't explored all that employers are looking for yet – all Seven Signs.

"Only then are you in a place to start writing it up, which is why I say a CV is the last thing you need. You have to cover everything else first. We still have one more of the Seven Signs to cover but we'll come back to that once you've had your first stab at a Clear Vision CV. I think you understand what I'm looking for."

Cheryl passed everyone a single sheet of paper with a template for a Clear Vision CV on it.

CLEAR VISION CV

My contact details
My personal statement
My skills & qualities – with examples
My summarised job history (relevant to the post I'm applying for)
Education & training (relevant to the post I'm applying for)
Personal interests (supporting the information above)

From lonely hearts to full page ads

Naz had his head down. He still was not convinced this was the best approach for employers but it was an interesting exercise. He could at least see how it looked by the end and add the good parts to his existing CV. Broken down into boxes like this, it was easier to build something from scratch and like everyone else, he started with his contact details and then copied his personal statement from the sheet of paper he'd been waving around earlier into the next space down.

Only one or two people noticed the door open. It was Rich and he asked Cheryl if he could have a word. She instructed the group to work through the sheet, box-by-box, and that they had half an hour.

"Ying, come and get me in the office if anyone needs me."

By the time Cheryl returned to the room, Naz had listed the six skills and qualities that he'd shortlisted earlier as the ones best for the campaigning job he had set his sights on. Now he had to put one sentence next to each, describing when he'd displayed that skill. He knew it had to be something that an employer would understand and find impressive.

Cheryl stood behind him and quietly asked how he was getting on.

"To be fair, Cheryl, I'm struggling," he replied frankly. "I have these six words but my mind's a bit blank when it comes to finding the right examples."

She stooped over the table and looked at his six shortlisted skills and qualities:

- Caring, compassionate people person
- Responsible
- Problem-solver
- Inspiring leader
- Goal-oriented project manager
- Committed to social justice

"Good list, Naz. What is your 'One Big Thing' again? You know, your long-term goal."

"I'm thinking something around campaigning on social justice. I'd love that, although I'm not entirely sure where to start. And I think I should be management but maybe not on day one," he joked.

Cheryl didn't laugh and Naz thought she seemed distracted, which was unlike her.

"You'll get there Naz. I think that's a good goal. You'd be good at that."

She stared at the shortlist for a while.

"Okay, so where shall we start? What about leadership? When do you think you have been an inspiring leader?"

"It's not a great example, Cheryl," he started. "It was when I was in prison, when I was mentoring the guys there. I think I inspired some of them."

"Might it depend on who you want a campaigning job with? What if it was, say, the Prison Reform Trust?"

"Oh, yeah…" Naz was intrigued. "I hadn't thought along those lines."

"Well…"

"Okay, here goes. *Working alongside offenders, I offered a counselling service to help them work through their issues and start planning for the future. People I worked with saw me as a role model because I had been in their situation and become successful.*"

"Good."

"I think I'd have to decide whether to mention… what did you call it? 'Lived experience,' depending on the job."

"Yep."

"Okay. I think I get what I need to do now."

"Look, nothing today is written in stone," Cheryl reassured Naz. "You can change and improve things over time, especially as you get feedback from employers."

She stood up and addressed the whole group.

"When you come onto the job history and education sections, remember we just want a summary. See how that looks. If you've had loads of jobs, don't try to squeeze them all in. After today, you can format your CV however you like but for my purposes, I only want to see a summary of information. The theory is that this will leave out the irrelevant information like gaps in your work history.

"As for interests, anything can go in that box but the things you talked about earlier would be ideal, the things you're passionate about.

"If you are applying for a job and working towards your 'One Big Thing,' your interests should be directly relevant. Focus on those as they will help make every part of your CV sell you. Put swimming if you want but if you like using Facebook and it's a computer-based role you're going for, include that."

Cheryl let them continue for another 10 minutes. As the coffee break approached, she wrapped up.

"For us, CV stands for Clear Vision. That's what you really need if you want to find work. Show an employer you know yourself and what you want from work. Now all you need is to type it up…"

She smiled.

"If I'd said to you we were going to create a CV from scratch in just a couple of hours, you would never have believed me, but now look. Just about all of you have a draft CV that I think really tells an employer what they need to know – how much you have to offer now and where you want to go in future."

Naz looked at his CV. Surely it couldn't be this simple. It wasn't as long as others he'd seen but he couldn't think of anything that was missing. He liked that it didn't make the gaps in his work history obvious, although that might come up at interview or in an application form, but as a positive place to start, this was different from what he had already. He might even try and mix the two together.

Navashen De

127 Charlton Road, Easton, Bristol, BS5 1UP
nazde89@gmail.com | 07875 876320

PERSONAL STATEMENT

As someone focused on a positive future and helping to create a better world, I want to put my people skills to use in a job where I can solve problems and offer some leadership in a management role. I am currently looking for a communications position for a campaigning charity where I can channel my commitment to social justice.

SKILLS AND QUALITIES

- **Caring, compassionate, people person:** I volunteer with a food outreach service, working as part of a team to provide meals and support to local homeless people
- **Responsible:** My current, temporary role requires me to oversee completion of jobs by a team, working to targets and deadlines, starting early or staying late if required to ensure each contract is delivered on time
- **Problem-solver:** As a mentor working with offenders, I researched information clients needed to support their efforts to sort out housing or deal with health issues, working through plans to help them
- **Inspiring leader:** Working well within a team and under my own initiative, colleagues often turn to me for direction. I have also led on publicity campaigns I devised for the charity I volunteer for
- **Goal-oriented project manager:** One PR drive was for food donations. By setting goals and breaking them down into smaller milestones, we worked towards achieving our target of having six months' worth of long-life produce
- **Committed to social justice:** Working with ex-offenders and rough sleepers, I have seen first-hand how people with potential miss out on opportunities in life because of poor choices or bad luck in the past. Through recent training, I have seen how open minds and structured support can create a fair society and I want to promote this

WORK AND EDUCATION (SUMMARY)
2010 to date (support roles)
Outreach, befriending and marketing work to support a project that delivers free food for rough sleepers in Bristol. Counselling offenders in prison, coaching them to adopt positive lifestyles.

Activity has included:
- Helping distribute meals to homeless people, including organising transport and overseeing food hygiene
- Talking customers through the support that is on offer and discussing their ambitions for the future
- Signposting individuals to specialist support
- Peer counselling, under supervision
- Mentoring offenders and helping motivate them to do well

2007 to date (various roles)
Various roles including delivery and fulfilment work for my current employer:

- Taking direction and working to instructions to pack and deliver materials around the city
- Leading teams of sessional workers, many of whom were long-term unemployed with challenging behaviour
- Customer service is a core part of the volunteer work I currently do with the food distribution charity – I believe quality should always be high enough that even paying customers would come back
- Seasonal work picking plants and vegetables

Education and training
- Digital Skills Course (2015) – Word, Excel, Email and Internet
- Food Hygiene Training (2015)
- Level 2 Certificate in Mentoring (2013)
Harlesden High School: 5 GCSEs, grades C-E

INTERESTS
I enjoy helping others and following current affairs, especially around human rights and social justice. I volunteer with a homelessness charity.

I'M READY

SIGN 7: MOTIVATION

News

"This is really not cool," Naz mumbled. "Not cool at all." He felt hot and cold at the same time and he couldn't focus his mind on anything.

Ying had bowed her head, trying to make sense of what Cheryl had just said, but she raised it to Naz.

"You okay?"

She looked at him, and watched him trying to look composed and strong. The harder he tried, she thought, the more he looked like a little boy.

"Naz, are you okay?"

Cheryl perched on the edge of the table facing the group. Part of her was relieved this had happened during the course, instead of after, because she could focus on the people in the room and push her own feelings to the back of her mind. Some people were carrying on like normal but she knew others would be reeling – you could just never tell who would be affected and how.

It was probably the hardest thing she'd had to do in her work life. Even knowing whether to tell the group or wait and tell some of them later had been a difficult call. She had talked it through with Rich before coming back to the training room. What she'd said was still fresh in her mind. It had been so hard to say.

Guys, if I could just have your attention for a moment. I'm sorry, you can return to the exercise in a moment. I'm afraid I have some sad news and I wanted you to hear it together. I've just found out that Jock died last night. We think it was a stroke but that's all we know at the moment. I'm really sorry, people.

The few seconds' silence after she'd spoken had been like torture. Cheryl did not feel emotional. She had a job to do and right now that was about managing the fallout among the group. Once the information sunk in, would they shrug it off or storm out the room? Would cocky Naz make some remark and start an argument? Would Alison put up her defences, returning to being negative and hopeless? Would Ying break down, confronted by death once more so soon after her father passed away?

Ali put her hand up to speak.

"Cheryl, do you think we could have just a ten minute break? A few of us could do with some fresh air.

We'll stay on later, if we don't finish."

Ali knew Ying and Naz well enough and could sense something was about to erupt if they couldn't get out of this space right now. Like Cheryl, she too had entered a different mode. It was like when her daughter fell off her scooter. She had to resist the temptation to rush in, terrified. Things would settle down much faster if she kept calm and watched out for whatever she could do to make things better.

Naz was already fishing anxiously for his tobacco in his coat pocket. He didn't even hear Cheryl approve Alison's suggestion because he was already up and walking towards the door. He hadn't really heard Ying asking after him either and was surprised she followed him out, along with Ali.

"Did you want to be alone?" Ying asked sensitively.

"Whatever."

"You seem upset."

"It is what it is. It's messed up. Everything always is."

Ali stood and listened. She didn't want to add to any drama. She just put a calming hand on his arm as he looked away into the distance. She turned to Ying and gestured to leave Naz alone for a moment and they began to talk between the two of them, while he stood in silence, smoking.

"This is crazy," Ying started. "It seems so unfair. I'm really shocked, you know."

"It is shocking," said Ali. "I wonder if it happens a lot around here. Cheryl didn't seem too phased."

"Maybe it comes with the job. I bet deep down she's really, really sad. I think she cares for all of us, I truly do. That's why she's staying strong but I am sure she is upset about…"

"Maybe it's not true," Naz interrupted hopefully. "He can't be dead."

"We can hope for the best," Ali responded, "but we should also prepare for the worst."

"I have had a lot of counselling about losing someone," Ying offered. "In the long term, it helps to accept things even if it's hard to start with, you know. Breathe and believe, my counsellor said all the time. Breathe and believe."

Ali noticed Naz drawing deep lungfuls of air. *He's listening,* she thought to herself. It seemed to her he no longer looked like he might cry.

But as Naz composed himself, he felt a sudden wave of anger. He needed to sort himself out and fast.

This is pathetic, he thought, *and why are these two here like a couple of mother hens?*

"Maybe you should splash your face with water, Naz," Ali suggested. "It's really hot out here."

He disappeared while she and Ying waited in silence. Both the men's and women's toilets were across the courtyard. He probably didn't realise, or didn't care, but they could hear Naz shouting "No, no, no, no, no."

Ying pulled a deliberately sad face in sympathy and now Ali placed a hand on her arm.

"He'll be okay," she said.

He returned a few minutes later to find them waiting at the foot of the iron stairs. He had taken their advice and put some cold water on his face, but he was also rubbing the knuckles of his right hand, now sore after punching the wall. He felt better for the release but knew it was a sign that he was not dealing with the setback.

"You okay?" Ying asked.

"Yeah, yeah."

They walked back to Seven Signs training, trying to calm their minds and focus on what they needed to do.

The Six Frogs

Cheryl looked around the group slowly.

"Now, does anyone have any objection to us moving onto the final part of the training?"

There was silence in the room.

"Guys?"

"I think we should, Cheryl," Ali said plainly.

"Naz, what about you?"

Naz threw his arms in the air. "What's the point?"

Ying leaned forward and put a hand on Naz's shoulder. "Naz, I know it's hard. We all liked Jock. He was getting on with his life. He knew what he wanted. Same as you."

She nodded to his CV and list of skills and qualities and then continued.

"Jock wouldn't want you to give up. Just like my

dad didn't want me to give up. And I'm going to try my hardest to make all this work."

The silence returned. Naz stared at the floor. Then he gave the tiniest of nods. Ying leaned back and managed a small smile at Cheryl, then wrote in the corner of the page in her notebook - *N and A mobile numbers/text meet for coffee.* She circled it. It seemed Ali would be fine but the three of them could help each other make sure the whole experience led onto better things. It had to.

"I'm going to start this final session with a riddle," Cheryl said. "Six frogs are sitting on a log and if five frogs decide to jump off, how many will be left?"

"It's got to be a trick."

"Of course, Naz, it's a riddle. But there's a point. How many are left?"

Ying put her hand up and called out. "It has to be one. One frog is left."

"Anyone else? No? The answer is six. Six are left. Just because five *decided* to jump off, doesn't mean anyone did anything."

"For goodness' sake," Naz muttered.

"I don't get it," Alison said.

"She means that just because we've worked out our goals, and listed our skills…" Naz started.

"And worked out what employers want…" Ying butted in.

"And practiced telling recruiters what is important to us…"

"And how good we are…"

"And learnt how to ask for help when we need it, don't forget," Cheryl added.

"It means nothing unless we actually do something about it," finished Ali.

Cheryl nodded. "Exactly. It's motivation. That's the last of the Seven Signs. You can display all the other six signs but they're not worth anything without the drive and motivation to use them."

SIGN 7 – MOTIVATION

When you show you are motivated, you:
- Prove you mean business about finding work
- Start to work towards your goals and your One Big Thing
- MAKE IT HAPPEN!

"Now," she added, "we bring it all together."

The Seven Signs come together

Cheryl turned over a sheet of flipchart paper on the stand at the front of the room to reveal the outline of a human body. It was strangely posed, not with its arms down but with one arm raised like it was hailing a cab.

Cheryl reached into her bag and withdrew seven

pieces of card.

"You gotta have vision. A clear vision. Remember *eyes*."

She stuck the word *VISION* just below the forehead on the diagram.

"Naz, what's your vision?"

"I want to work in a comms role for a campaigning charity…"

"Great," Cheryl interrupted. "To identify the right job goal, which gives you clear vision, you have to know what skills you have. I remember this one as a hand, or 'something you can put your hand to.'" She stuck *SKILLS* to the hand hanging down to the body outline's side.

"Ali, give me three skills."

"Erm, organised, compassionate, self-disciplined…"

"Okay," Cheryl said, without looking away from the flipchart. "And that should also reflect your passion. Where should passion go? I'd put it here, on the heart." She stuck *PASSION* across the chest.

"Fairness and social justice," shouted Naz, without being asked.

"What else do we have? Ah, yes, 'asking for help.' Well, you want to know why this jobseeker looks like he's waving at someone in the street? It's because he…"

"Or she," Naz shouted.

"Or she is asking for help." *ASKING FOR HELP* went onto the raised hand.

"Asking for help. Ying? An example?"

"Telling an employer I might need time out sometimes for health reasons. Saying I have an appointment, trying to give them notice."

"Exactly." Cheryl turned to face the group. "Now, I got a little stuck with the next one. But I think 'What employers want' is knowledge and that can only really go in your brain, so I'll put this one up here."

She had to move the *VISION* tag down slightly to make room but Cheryl slapped *WHAT EMPLOYERS WANT* onto the forehead.

"And what do they want?"

Naz jumped in. "All of the above?"

"Well, yes. And the below. All the Seven Signs."

Cheryl was motoring through.

"Next, I have this one..." She placed PRESENTATION at the bottom of the figure's face.

"It has to be where the mouth is, right? It represents how you'll *tell* employers that you have what they're looking for but that means on paper in your personal statement and on your CV, as well as verbally in interview or on the street, if you get the chance."

Ying jumped in. "So, vision is knowing your personal statement and presentation is being able to say it or write it?"

Ali felt there was slightly more to it.

"And being able to build on it, using the statement as the foundation, but describing it and backing it up with examples."

"Excellent," Cheryl said. "So, what's left everybody?"

There was quiet.

"Come on. Six frogs on a log because they lack…" Up went *MOTIVATION*. "I think this goes on the feet because it's about you having the drive to go places, and that's what your feet do."

There was a stunned silence.

Ali was thinking, *what just happened?*

"That's it. The Seven Signs."

Cheryl looked triumphant and everyone was nodding but what *had* just happened?

"Guys, does that make sense?"

Ali called out: "It does. Has the course really all been leading up to this?"

"Pretty much. These Seven Signs of job readiness are how employers know you're the right people to offer paid work to. You have shown them something – something that all employers look for, often without realising. We think they really know the right person when they meet them because those people switch on the Seven Signs.

"Good candidates are self-possessed. By that I mean that the jobseeker has an air of confidence about them. It just says 'I won't let you down because I'm the right person for this job and if I get stuck, I'll ask for help.' Make sense?"

Everyone nodded.

"Right, you have one last task before you leave. And once you've written down three things you're actually going to do in the next fortnight, you can leave. I want you to write it down twice – one list you'll leave with me and one you'll take with you. I'm going to call you in two weeks and one day to find out how you're doing. Remember what we said about building your own ladders and creating your own luck. Now you're going to get started, if you haven't already."

Cheryl handed out a list called the *20 Next Steps for Jobseekers*, with 20 steps jobseekers could take to find, apply for, and win the right job for them. She explained they could write down three tasks of their own or use three of the *20 Next Steps.*

"All that matters is that you complete them within the next two weeks," she said.

SEVEN SIGNS OF JOB READINESS

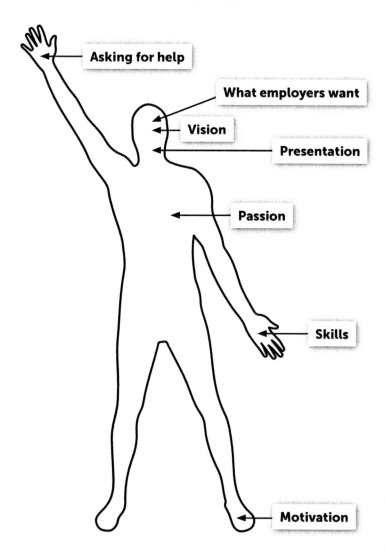

20 NEXT STEPS FOR JOBSEEKERS

If nothing else has really worked for you before now, why not try a slightly new approach? There are some simple steps you can take for yourself and tasks to try out on your own. They're pretty straightforward. What do you have to lose?

There is also a Seven Signs training website you can visit for more information and help along the way. Visit 7signs.org.uk to find hidden extras and tools to help you reach your goals.

1. *Taming the snakes*

It's sometimes easier to identify what is holding us back than what will help us succeed. People often hide behind barriers but by naming them and seeing them for what they are, we can start to work out how to overcome them. What are the snakes that seem to be lying in wait for you, ready to take you back away from your job goals? Is it meeting people – are you shy? Are you scared of your past catching up with you?

Whatever it is, write it down. Now ask yourself: "Is it that big a deal?" If it is, ask for help. Talk to someone about it and try to come to terms with it or even turn it into a positive, or make a strategy to work around it. Note down three snakes and list all you can do to stop them stopping you.

2. *Eyes on the prize*
It's almost impossible to score a goal if you don't know what goal you're aiming for. Everything gets easier once you've set one. Ask yourself what your dream job is. It doesn't matter if what comes up turns out to be right or wrong. It's a starting point and even the wrong goal will tell you a lot about what the right one might be. To work out if it's the best goal to go for, continue following this list of 20 tips to discover your One Big Thing.

3. *You're in charge*
It's really helpful to try thinking like an employer. Practice by taking a look at the three personal statements we included in the section on 'What Employers Want.' If you were recruiting a receptionist, which one would you choose and why? Note down what you like less about the other two. If you're online, go to the 7signs.org.uk website and download the role play job description and score sheet and give each candidate a mark out of five against each of the indicators.

4. *The good times say so much*

Write down the best thing you've achieved and the best role you ever had. Now add what it was about them that you enjoyed or made you proud. Are there any clues about what you might like to do for a job hidden in this information? This background information is useful for understanding what roles would get you motivated and may come in handy at interview when an employer asks for examples of when you've used your skills and qualities.

5. *The (wo)man in the mirror*

What makes you happy or angry or motivated? Think about what you look forward to or, again, the things you are proudest about having done. Where do your passions lie? Sport or politics or learning? Children or animals or other people? Making money, making sales or making people happy? Ask your friends and family. Write down what you're really into because it's what makes you *you*, and employers want to meet the real you and see if their job is right for you… and that you're right for their job.

6. *Skills, not spills*

Choose a friend or family member (or a stranger, for that matter, as they will tell you what they think, not what they think you want to hear) and tell them what you decided were the best things you've done. Based only on this information, ask them (or yourself) what they imagine you're like. Write down the long list of skills and qualities they come up with. See 7signs.org.uk for some examples.

7. *Short is sweet*

Take the long list of skills and qualities offered by your friends (or that you came up with yourself) and shorten the list to five or six that you really believe describe you best. Start thinking of examples when you used them.

8. *Window shop for jobs*

Now you've started to think about the jobs that could use your skills and reflect your interests, shop around. If you're new to the internet, it's a great way to learn how much it can do for you. Ask someone to show you – it's not brain surgery. Take down the details of as many employers with the right jobs as you can. Clarify what those employers want.

9. *Going round in circles*

Look at the One Big Thing template with three overlapping circles on it (you can download it from 7signs.org.uk). Filling it in will remind you of what makes you different from the next person competing for the same job as you. Use it to pin down the job you really want, produce a personal statement, write a CV and prepare for interview. Here are some useful steps to follow:

    a.   Write the skills you (or your friend or that

      stranger) identified into the top left hand circle that has the question 'What are you good at?' (See Step 6 above)

b.   Put the list of things that you care most about into the one labelled 'What do you enjoy doing?' (See Step 5 above)

c.   Add as many employers as you can find into the circle labelled 'What jobs can you apply for?' Don't worry if you may not be qualified for some or if they may exclude you because of your background (health or criminal record, for example). (See Step 8 above)

d.   Now, to complete the exercise, put the jobs you could definitely apply for that match your skills and passions in the curvy triangle space in the centre. These are the jobs to aim for, your One Big Thing.

10. *Let's get personal*

Using the template below if you need to, draft your own personal statement. Use just two or three of the most relevant skills and qualities from your shortlist. You can also include what you're passionate about, if it's right for the employers you'll be approaching. Include the job you're going for now and show you're motivated by saying what you are working towards.

> As someone with [x, y, z skills/qualities],
> I am seeking [first step job opportunity] to
> develop my skills and experience,
> working towards [my One Big Thing/long-term
> job goal].

11. *Start building your own ladders*

By knowing what you're looking for and having your personal statement prepared, you can make your own luck and build your own ladders towards your goals. You may not be approached in the street but you could bump into someone useful or a friend might mention something or you might see an ad in a shop window. Be on your guard for an opportunity. Make a note of where you might look or ask around.

12. *Get on with IT*

There is almost no job out there that won't need you to use a computer at some point or another – and you'll often need to use one during the application process. So, if you're not confident with IT, now is the time to grow your skills. You cannot break the internet and the basic skills are easy to pick up with practice – just get on with it.

    a.   If you don't have one, start by setting up an appropriate email address that won't put an employer off before you've even started.

Practice sending yourself emails that look more like letters than text messages, which is what employers will expect. Learn how to add attachments, like your CV.

b.   Get familiar with Microsoft Word by drafting a simple poster, playing with fonts, size and colour. Draft a letter and now type up your CV. Find the spellchecker and get into the habit of using it. Always.

c.   Practice filling in online forms, like surveys, and register with Facebook and LinkedIn, which will help you grow your confidence and practice sharing information.

d.   Search online for things you're passionate about – this helps grow the same skills you'll need to search for vacancies.

13: *20:20 foresight*

C is for Clear and V is for Vision. To prepare for producing your CV, return to your shortlist of 5-6 skills and qualities (see Step 7 above). In no more than one short sentence, give the best example of when you used that skill or displayed that quality. Remember, this is for an employer, so think about what will impress them most, bearing in mind the job you're going for.

14: *More than the sum of your past*

List all the dates of your schooling, education and training, then summarise them on no more than five lines. Now list your job history just summarising the experience you have and highlighting the roles and tasks you had to do that demonstrate you have the skills and qualities you will need for the job(s) you're applying for now.

15. *Be clear, have vision – your CV*
On a single page (if possible, but two pages is fine) type:
   a.   Your contact details
   b.   Personal statement
   c.   Your list of skills/qualities supported with examples
   d.   A summary of your education and work history
   e.   Two or three lines on your interests and what gets you going

Use your IT skills to format it well and email it to yourself. Ask people to look it over and tell you how it could be improved (you can download a template and see examples on 7signs.org.uk).

16. *Devil is in the detail*
Look hard at the job description before you apply for work. Be sure you have the right skills. If you don't, think about how you'll reassure the employer you can do the job and if you struggle with that, consider if it's really the right job for you right now. Find a job description for your dream job and do the same. If you'll need training, think about starting it as soon as possible, even if you have to do other jobs in the meantime, especially if the

Job Centre is on your back about coming off benefits.

17. *Turning tables*
What do *you* want from an employer? You know what you're working towards in the future, so prepare a few questions of your own to ask them at interview. This shows you mean business about doing well in the job and also helps you decide if they're the right employer for you (even if you don't feel you can be too choosy right now).

18. *Disclosure for closure*
Practice what you'd say if an employer asked you to explain a health issue or a criminal record that might make them think twice about employing you. If you have no skeletons in your closet, think of weaknesses a tough interviewer might quiz you on. Write down three points you can make that will reassure them that it will not be a problem for you – or them – or get in the way of you doing well in the job.

19. *Put yourself out there*
It can be daunting to say to the world 'come and find me' but it shows confidence and it helps employers find you.
   a.   Practice with LinkedIn. Create a profile and include everything you put together for your CV. Then copy the link to your profile and include it in emails and on your CV.

b. Register with recruitment agencies, especially the ones filling jobs in the industry you've set your sights on. Chase them every week. Don't wait for them to call you, as they will almost always turn to people they think of first, which will be the people they hear from most.

c. Join as many job websites as you can find, uploading your CV to each one. Create a routine for browsing the jobs every couple of days and apply for all the suitable ones, trying to make your application even better each time.

d. Put out 'your feelers' using social media like Facebook, Twitter and LinkedIn. Look up employers you want to work for, and regularly check their social media spaces and their website, to be ahead of the game when they're recruiting. What you learn about them will also come in handy at interview.

e. Ask around and contact bosses who may have work in future. If they don't have work right now, ask who might and tell *that* person they were recommended by the person who gave you their contact details.

20. *Steel yourself*

Jobseeking is a sales job and any person who works in sales will tell you that success is about accepting you will be turned down. Treat every 'no' as a 'not this time.' Understand why they didn't want you and prepare to deal with it next time. Remember, not every job is right for you and a 'no' may actually take you a step closer to the right one.

Remember the Six Frogs riddle

There are six frogs sitting on a log. Five decide to jump off but unless they follow through, six frogs remain sitting on a log going nowhere. Write down three actions from this list that you will take in the next two weeks to move closer to your long-term job goal(s). Tell someone you trust and ask them to check in with you on the date two weeks from today.

You've decided to jump, now jump!

I'M READY

MOVING ON

Naz gets a gentle push

Rain was pattering onto the skylight window and Rich's office was looking more dingy than usual. Alison was alone there with a sheet that had the names and contact details of all the people who had started Seven Signs training.

She looked down the list, putting a tick next to Antonio's name, who she had just spoken to on the phone. Cheryl had asked Ali to complete the ring round as part of her paid time as a support worker. She placed a small cross next to Jock's name, a lump forming in her throat.

She picked up the phone and dialled Naz.

"Naz? How are you?"

They made small talk over the phone for a short while and then she explained Cheryl had asked her to call everyone to see how they were progressing with the three steps they said they'd take in the two weeks since the course.

"I really didn't think anyone would actually call," Naz replied, surprised.

"Well, it's just me. Have you done anything?" She picked up the crinkled sheet of paper he'd left after the final session of the course.

"It says here you would get onto LinkedIn and reconnect with people you used to work with in prison, pin down examples of your skillset and update your CV with skills and examples of work experience."

"Well, I haven't exactly written anything down…"

"Have you done anything?"

"I have mentioned what I'm looking for to a couple of people."

"Okay. How did that go?"

"Nothing yet. I kind of lost momentum. I mean, don't you ask yourself what's the point? It's like I said in our last meeting…" His voice tailed off. Ali could hear him breathing.

Alison knew what he was thinking. "I know Jock's death hit you hard, Naz. There will always be setbacks. We have to choose if they'll knock us off course or make us stronger. I know we were talking about job rejections when we discussed setbacks, but…"

"It's not the same, Ali."

"Isn't it? What do you think is going to happen round here? Rich says we've lost seven people since he started Seven Signs training. If each one doesn't make you want to try harder, for everyone else, then I guess you'd be right, there's no point. You gotta brush yourself down and get back on that bike, Naz."

"You make me feel like a complete loser."

"Your words, not mine."

There was silence for a moment, then Naz spoke, his voice hard with resolve. "I will. I will sort it out."

"Right. So, how about I book a time for you to come in and we can work it through together? How long do you actually think those things will take?"

Naz was impressed. What happened to the negative girl hiding behind excuses for finding work? It seemed a bit unfair that it was her chasing him – she knew only too well what it was like and she was less likely to take 'no' for an answer.

Curse you, Cheryl, he wanted to say, joking.

"I guess it won't actually take that long once I get down to it. When are you next in?"

"Day after tomorrow? How about 10.30 when I get in after the school run?" She wrote his name in the desk diary. "You can do this, Naz. You know you can. You just need to crack on, so let's do it."

"And how are you getting on, mate?"

Ali was a little taken aback. She had to think for a second.

"Well, it's like everything has changed. I'm waiting to hear back from three applications I put in and one agency who seemed keen. It's rubbish pay but it's experience. There's a real shortage of people to work in care homes. Everything's happening at once. I'm moving into a flat next week."

"Ali, you know that's not a coincidence, right?" He waited but she didn't say anything. "That's you making your own luck."

"Do you think so? I was never convinced..."

"Me neither but what can I say, you're doing it. Building your own ladders."

They continued chatting for a couple of minutes. After the call, Naz was determined. He would meet Ali and try to work through more of the list than he'd already committed to. Ali was on the move and, he realised, if he wasn't careful he'd be left behind.

I need to make like those frogs, Naz thought to himself.

Later he dug out the list of *20 Next Steps for Jobseekers* he might consider. There were some he would look at first because they seemed easier, which would feel like progress. Other actions needed to be done in turn, once other things were in place.

It felt like time to get down to business.

Raising a toast

"Ying texted me earlier," said Ali. "We're going to meet for a coffee later. She's not been feeling too good and wanted to catch up. She said she wants to leave some flowers in remembrance for Jock."

Naz looked back at Ali blankly. "Do people do that?"

"Sounds like Ying does. It's kind of nice. I think it's

more for her than him, so she can do what she feels is right and then move on. I want to see if she's ready to come back in and give things another go."

Naz asked if it was okay to join them and was pleased Ali agreed.

"Actually," he added, "can you set me up at a computer? I need to type up a new CV and want to email it to a couple of people to see if they have jobs going."

Naz spent the following hour typing up what he'd written out on a sheet of paper that looked like he had been carrying it around for months, not days. He asked Ali to look over the finished article on screen before he emailed it to himself, so he could send it on to anyone from anywhere. She told him it looked good to her apart from a couple of spelling mistakes that he corrected straight away.

Naz started researching charities in the local area. His first search came back with over a hundred organisations, so he refined it to *charity campaigns Bristol*, which gave him around thirty. He printed them off, then crossed through those working with animals and religious ones, which were not for him.

Back on screen, he clicked through to the dozen or so that remained on his shortlist and tried to find the HR or senior management contacts, writing the email details on his printout. Before drafting the email he planned to send to each one, he re-read his personal statement. Then he had a crack at writing his first email.

Dear Ms Divandra,

I am writing to ask if your organisation is currently recruiting for any communications, campaigns or marketing roles.

As you will see from the CV attached, I am committed to positive change and looking for the chance to put my responsible and compassionate nature to use in a job where I can put my leadership and project management skills into practice.

I have spent a long time reflecting on my longer-term goals and identified that an organisation like yours is exactly where I would like to develop a career. I am currently out of work and would be happy to discuss a voluntary role, if it can help take me towards my job goals.

I have a particular interest in your charity's goals, having had first-hand experience of the issues, although not in the past three years. More recently, I have worked on a voluntary basis with some of your customers who are homeless in the city.

I look forward to hearing from you and would be grateful for any feedback or advice you can give me about ways I could find this kind of work with you or similar organisations, including an idea of where you usually advertise vacancies.

Yours sincerely,

Naz De

"It was weird," Naz said later, while stirring his tea. "I started to see each email I lined up as a frog jumping off a log. That Cheryl really gets inside your head."

They had ordered food and Ying was hungry.

"It's good you're doing that, Naz." She attempted a smile but she felt tired and knew that it looked half-hearted. She looked down, hoping he didn't notice.

"How many did you send off in the end?" said Ali. She had noticed Ying was struggling and already knew that the past few weeks had set her back a little. On the phone, Ali had been encouraging and supportive, reminding Ying she should take her time and not push herself too hard.

When Jock passed away, it had stirred up some of the feelings Ying had felt when her father died, but now she was here, things just needed to be as normal as possible. They could focus on Naz as he was usually happy to be the centre of attention.

"I sent five. It took longer than I'd expected because they all do slightly different things, so I had to make sure what I was saying made sense."

He was honestly proud of himself and upbeat about his chances of finding something that he actually wanted to do.

"I've a few more to do but I definitely will. A friend has a laptop I can use and I'll be in next time the office is open. Then I just need to remind myself that I'm only looking for one 'yes' and that I can't get disheartened when the majority of emails I get back are a 'no.'"

"It's hard, though," Ying agreed.

"If it was easy, we'd all be in a job," Ali reminded them.

"Too right, mate. And I think on that note," added Naz brightly, "we should raise a non-alcoholic toast to Jock."

"Yes. Let's do that. Let's make something positive of this," Ying said.

They raised their cups and clinked them, smiling but drifting off into memories of Jock and thoughts of what the future held.

Rich & Cheryl wrap up

Rich and Cheryl were finishing off the paperwork for Seven Signs training. They had funders to keep happy and had put together a pack of information about the number of attendees and the progress each had made towards finding work and taking control of issues that could be holding them back.

"We done?" Rich checked.

Cheryl counted the small stack of folders that would be filed at a later date and nodded.

"Still on for a drink?"

"Absolutely. I have a pass for a couple of hours. I think we've earned it on this one."

They locked up and headed to the Full Moon pub along the road and through a gateway in a stone wall that few people knew existed. It was late afternoon and the pub was quiet. They took a table by the window that looked out onto the main street. Rich brought over two large glasses of white wine.

"Well," Cheryl ventured as Rich sat down, "to Jock then?"

"To Jock."

"Do you think he'd approve of us drinking to him?"

"I can see him grinning that cheeky grin."

"What an absolute star." Cheryl began to think about the others in the group. "That was the hardest thing I think I've ever had to do, breaking that news."

"I know," Rich said, staring out the window, so he avoided Cheryl's eyes. "Poor Jock."

"I wish it hadn't been on my watch."

"C'mon," Rich replied. "I'm glad it was. You could make sure everyone was okay."

"Maybe. But that's what was hard. How have they been?"

"Mostly good. Naz came in this morning and did a shedload of emails. Ali's a different person altogether."

"What about Ying?"

"I've been coaching Ali through that one. I think she's the perfect person to just keep contact. A light-touch approach. She'll be fine, I think. We'll keep an eye on her."

They chatted casually about how the business was going, big ideas for the future, and where the money would come from to continue Seven Signs training.

Then Cheryl said, "And what about you? How are

you doing?"

"Ah, you know…"

"I wouldn't have asked if I did."

"Honestly? I think I need a break." He stopped and recognised one of those pauses each of them left when talking to the jobseekers. "I wonder if there should be eight signs, with the last one being 'dealing with setbacks.' When I found out about Jock, it felt like everything was suddenly too much, like there's someone somewhere just trying to mess everything up. I know how these guys feel, you know? How do they keep going?"

Cheryl gently put a hand on his arm. "You have to watch out for yourself. We can't have you burning out. You do sound like you need a break." She smiled at him kindly but he was looking away. "And by the way, it's because you know how they feel that all this works. It's called empathy. That's why they trust you."

"It just feels like…"

"Like you don't have control?" Cheryl watched him as he stared out to the busy stream of traffic outside. "We don't have control over everything, Rich. You know that. And that's why we don't need an eighth sign – the seven do just fine. And do you know why?"

Rich didn't answer but Cheryl could tell he was listening.

"You'll be fine because you know you only need to ask for help." She didn't want to sound like his mother. "You know there are people you can turn to. Like me.

And there are people you can lean on, like everyone who comes in to see us every day, who know what you've done for them. They're just looking for the chance to repay you somehow. You might not open up to them but you know you can call on them. Just look at Ali, for goodness' sake."

They sat in silence for a few moments.

"I'll be back in a sec," Rich mumbled as he stood and disappeared to the toilet. When he returned, he had composed himself and felt much better.

"Thanks, Cheryl," he said as he sat down. "This is just what I needed. And you're totally right."

"Of course. I always am," she joked, laughing.

Au revoir, Naz

"You around for a bit?" Naz said to Rich when he came in to collect his wage slip. "I could do with a word."

"Sure." Rich watched Naz open the brown envelope and read the contents. "Bumper week, isn't it? Your biggest payment yet."

"Yeah, it's been going good. Good to get the team leader rate too."

"You earned it. It's been noted how you've been putting your back into the work recently. Not like in the beginning, eh?" Rich smiled as he watched Naz squirm a little, remembering his attitude in the first few sessions with Cheryl. "Walk with me. I need to go grab a sandwich."

The two of them descended the iron staircase towards the café at the bottom.

"So, what's up Naz?"

Naz was suddenly very nervous and stuttered as he began to speak. "I've got some news and I feel bad now, having just opened my payslip. It's good and bad news."

"Just say it. It's the only way."

Naz stopped at the café door to look Rich square in the eye. "Well, the thing is… I've been offered a job."

"Naz! Amazing!" Rich grinned.

"You sure you're happy with that?" Naz questioned, not sure how he felt about Rich being happy to see him go. "I feel bad. It's full-time and I won't be able to stay on here. I'm really sorry. I feel like I'm letting you down."

"Don't be a dumbass," Rich quipped. "That's how it's supposed to work. I told you from the start I didn't want to see you here forever."

"I assumed you meant you didn't want me hanging around."

"Well, there was that but only for the old Naz. It's just bloody typical that as soon as you work out what I need from you, you go and find work." Rich looked Naz in the eye. "But seriously, I'm chuffed for you. If I didn't want you moving on into regular employment, I wouldn't be doing a very good job myself, would I?"

"But who's going to…"

"Not your worry, fella. How many people have you worked with over the past few weeks?"

Naz thought for a while. It had been a busy time, which was why he'd earned so much.

"Well, there must have been about 20 pay envelopes for people upstairs."

"So, then, I have at least 20 people to offer a promotion to. They can't be any more difficult than you were when you started." Rich saw Naz's smile drop from his face. "I'm messing with you, fella."

Rich asked about the new job. It was with a volunteering project for a cancer charity. Naz explained he had completed some awareness training and a couple of 'try-out' sessions, and now he would take on a junior admin role in the communications team.

"They say 'team' but it's actually just me and this guy who is planning to move up north in the new year, so I'm hoping I can impress them enough to step into his shoes."

They chatted as Rich ordered a sandwich and as they left the café, Ali and Cheryl turned the corner into the cobbled courtyard. They were both weighed down with bags full of paper.

"Naz has some news," Rich said, as his mobile phone started ringing. "I'll let him explain and catch you all later… hey Antonio, ça va?" He headed back up the metal steps. "Woah, woah, woah. I can't really speak French. In English, in English. Great, great. Listen, I've got some work I might need you for…"

Naz told the women about the job and Cheryl gave him a hug that embarrassed him, partly because it made him feel like an awkward teenager and partly because he remembered the day he'd first met the woman. He had to admit he could have handled that first time better. He wanted to apologise but the moment had passed.

"Cheryl, erm, I want to thank you."

"Don't be silly."

"But…"

"Hey, I get paid to do this. And it's the job I jump out of bed for, remember? I don't do it for thanks."

She hugged him again, though, knowing it was freaking him out.

"Ali, this'll be you next time. She's my apprentice now, Naz. She's going to run some of the course for me."

"You'll be great at that, Ali."

"Thanks."

"Let's hope you don't get anyone like me on your first day."

"Bring it on," said Alison boldly. "You're not so scary, Naz. Not really. And if I do see anyone like that, I'll just think of you and how you wear your game face. It's not really you. That's what Ying says." She grinned.

"How is Ying?" Naz asked.

"Not so good, if I'm honest. But she will be. I'm going to ask her to give me a hand and I think she'll see she's perfectly capable. She just needs to build her confidence. We'll get her there."

"She's displaying all the Seven Signs," said Cheryl.

"She just needs to prove to herself that she's ready.

"Right," she added. "Good to see you, Naz, and congratulations on the job. You won't look back. You're ready. Now we'd better crack on, Ali. You ready?"

"I'm ready."

About the author: Jeff Mitchell

Jeff Mitchell is the founder of community enterprise Clean Slate Training & Employment, 're-activating' long-term unemployed people since 2006 through paid work experience, formal training (Seven Signs) and peer support. Clean Slate specialises in working with people with histories of homelessness, mental health issues and offending, as well as refugees. Jeff also runs the Social Publishing Project, which produces money management materials for people on low incomes. He was previously managing director of The Big Issue, the magazine sold by homeless people, where he came to recognise that everyone has the potential for success if given the right support and opportunity. Jeff is a keen runner and active blogger and can be found on LinkedIn at **https://uk.linkedin.com/in/jeffmitchelluk**.

About the editor: J M Lawrence

J M Lawrence is an award-winning journalist and New York Times bestselling author based in Bristol, UK. He has been writing and editing for 20 years and has worked in a range of related areas including copywriting and content strategy. He is currently employed as managing editor for a portfolio of business websites. When not planning his next great novel or actually writing the damn thing, he enjoys playing sports, mindfulness, connecting with nature and spending time with his fiancée Sophie. He can be found online at **www.jmlawrence.co.uk**.